WATER

OPPOSING VIEWPOINTS®

Other Books of Related Interest in the Opposing Viewpoints Series:

Africa
Animal Rights
The Environmental Crisis
Genetic Engineering
Global Resources
The Health Crisis
The Middle East
The Third World

WATER

OPPOSING VIEWPOINTS®

David L. Bender & Bruno Leone, *Series Editors*

Carol Wekesser, *Book Editor*

OPPOSING
VIEWPOINTS
SERIES®

Greenhaven Press, Inc.   PO Box 289009   San Diego, CA 92198-9009

Library of Congress Cataloging-in-Publication Data

Water : opposing viewpoints / Carol Wekesser, book editor.
   p.   cm. — (Opposing viewpoints series)
  Includes bibliographical references and index.
  Summary: Presents opposing viewpoints on issues relating to water, including managing the water supply, acid rain, and government regulations.
  ISBN 1-56510-064-6 (alk. paper). — ISBN 1-56510-063-8 (pbk. : alk. paper)
  1. Water-supply—Management. 2. Acid rain—Environmental aspects. 3. Water—Law and legislation. 4. Water quality management. 5. Critical thinking. [1. Water supply. 2. Water—Pollution. 3. Pollution.] I. Wekesser, Carol, 1963-   . II. Series: Opposing viewpoints series (Unnumbered)
TD348.W38 1994
333.91—dc20   93-12374
                                                    CIP
                                                     AC

"Congress shall make no law . . .
abridging the freedom of speech,
or of the press."

First Amendment to the U.S. Constitution

The basic foundation of our democracy is the first amendment
guarantee of freedom of expression. The Opposing Viewpoints
Series is dedicated to the concept of this basic freedom and the
idea that it is more important to practice it than to enshrine it.

Contents

Why Consider Opposing Viewpoints?

> *"The only way in which a human being can make some approach to knowing the whole of a subject is by hearing what can be said about it by persons of every variety of opinion and studying all modes in which it can be looked at by every character of mind. No wise man ever acquired his wisdom in any mode but this."*
>
> John Stuart Mill

In our media-intensive culture it is not difficult to find differing opinions. Thousands of newspapers and magazines and dozens of radio and television talk shows resound with differing points of view. The difficulty lies in deciding which opinion to agree with and which "experts" seem the most credible. The more inundated we become with differing opinions and claims, the more essential it is to hone critical reading and thinking skills to evaluate these ideas. Opposing Viewpoints books address this problem directly by presenting stimulating debates that can be used to enhance and teach these skills. The varied opinions contained in each book examine many different aspects of a single issue. While examining these conveniently edited opposing views, readers can develop critical thinking skills such as the ability to compare and contrast authors' credibility, facts, argumentation styles, use of persuasive techniques, and other stylistic tools. In short, the Opposing Viewpoints Series is an ideal way to attain the higher-level thinking and reading skills so essential in a culture of diverse and contradictory opinions.

In addition to providing a tool for critical thinking, Opposing Viewpoints books challenge readers to question their own strongly held opinions and assumptions. Most people form their opinions on the basis of upbringing, peer pressure, and personal, cultural, or professional bias. By reading carefully balanced opposing views, readers must directly confront new ideas as well as the opinions of those with whom they disagree. This is not to simplistically argue that everyone who reads opposing views will—or should—change his or her opinion. Instead, the series enhances readers' depth of understanding of their own views by encouraging confrontation with opposing ideas. Careful examination of others' views can lead to the readers' understanding of the logical inconsistencies in their own opinions, perspective on why they hold an opinion, and the consideration of the possibility that their opinion requires further evaluation.

Evaluating Other Opinions

To ensure that this type of examination occurs, Opposing Viewpoints books present all types of opinions. Prominent spokespeople on different sides of each issue as well as well-known professionals from many disciplines challenge the reader. An additional goal of the series is to provide a forum for other, less known, or even unpopular viewpoints. The opinion of an ordinary person who has had to make the decision to cut off life support from a terminally ill relative, for example, may be just as valuable and provide just as much insight as a medical ethicist's professional opinion. The editors have two additional purposes in including these less known views. One, the editors encourage readers to respect others' opinions—even when not enhanced by professional credibility. It is only by reading or listening to and objectively evaluating others' ideas that one can determine whether they are worthy of consideration. Two, the inclusion of such viewpoints encourages the important critical thinking skill of objectively evaluating an author's credentials and bias. This evaluation will illuminate an author's reasons for taking a particular stance on an issue and will aid in readers' evaluation of the author's ideas.

As series editors of the Opposing Viewpoints Series, it is our hope that these books will give readers a deeper understanding of the issues debated and an appreciation of the complexity of even seemingly simple issues when good and honest people disagree. This awareness is particularly important in a democratic society such as ours in which people enter into public debate to determine the common good. Those with whom one disagrees should not be regarded as enemies but rather as people whose views deserve careful examination and may shed light on one's own.

Thomas Jefferson once said that "difference of opinion leads to inquiry, and inquiry to truth." Jefferson, a broadly educated man, argued that "if a nation expects to be ignorant and free . . . it expects what never was and never will be." As individuals and as a nation, it is imperative that we consider the opinions of others and examine them with skill and discernment. The Opposing Viewpoints Series is intended to help readers achieve this goal.

David L. Bender & Bruno Leone,
Series Editors

Introduction

"When the well's dry, we know the worth of water."

Benjamin Franklin

Water is the most abundant substance in the world. It comprises most of the human body and covers 72 percent of the earth. It is a seemingly endless resource that is so common people usually give little thought to it. Yet it is so valuable that people sometimes fight over it.

In the twentieth century, humans have used water to transform deserts into lush landscapes and to propel industry. For example, farmers in California's fertile Imperial Valley use Colorado River water to help generate about a billion dollars a year in livestock, grain, and produce. The valley, which receives only three inches of rainfall a year, would be a desert without irrigation from the river. Some California farmers even irrigate their land to grow rice, one of the world's most water-dependent crops.

For years, no one questioned this use of water as excessive—it was assumed that water was so plentiful that no concern was warranted. In recent decades, however, Americans have become increasingly aware that the water supply is not limitless nor immune to pollutants. Consequently, people are reevaluating the worth of water and attempting to create policies that will protect the water supply and ensure that all those who depend on clean water—people, wildlife, agriculture, industry—have access to it.

Part of this reevaluation is understanding that some of the old methods for procuring water—diverting and damming rivers and tapping into groundwater, for example—are harming wildlife or causing other long-term environmental problems. For example, for decades Great Plains farmers have depended upon the Ogallala Aquifer to irrigate their crops. But overuse is draining this underground source of water, once thought to be inexhaustible. Draining the aquifer drains the rivers and wetlands that feed it, irreparably altering wildlife habitats and endangering species. Dams similarly destroy canyons and river habitats.

While some farmers and environmentalists are finding methods to conserve groundwater and river water, others are exploring new ways of acquiring clean water. Saudi Arabia and other oil-rich, water-poor Persian Gulf states, for example, depend on desalinated seawater for about 50 percent of their industrial and domestic water needs. Desalination, although expensive, has also been touted as a solution for arid regions in the United States. As Kurt Stehling, senior scientist emeritus for the National Oceanic and Atmospheric Administration, states: "It is obvious that a rapidly increasing world population, coupled with uncertain rainfall patterns, leaves no choice but to find ways to economically remove the inimical substances in ocean or brackish water."

Desalination may indeed be the answer to some regions' water shortages. Many environmentalists and water experts, however, believe that new sources of water alone cannot solve the problems of water supply and water pollution. Only when people understand the true value of water will they willingly protect and conserve it. As Sandra Postel, author of *The Last Oasis: Facing Water Scarcity,* states, "Many of the water shortages cropping up around the world stem from the widespread failure to value water at anything close to its true worth." This inability or unwillingness to value water, she believes, "fosters waste and the planting of water-intensive crops" and prevents Americans from supporting water projects with tax money.

Regardless of what measures people decide to employ to conserve and protect water, the main issue is that water is vital to life on earth and consequently must be treasured. *Water: Opposing Viewpoints* evaluates how people use and abuse water, and what measures should be taken to protect it. Chapters include: How Should the Water Supply Be Managed? How Can Water Pollution Be Reduced? How Serious a Problem Is Acid Rain? How Serious a Problem Is Ocean Pollution? As Postel concludes:

> Modern society has come to view water only as a resource that is there for the taking, rather than a life-support system that underpins the natural world we depend on. Instead of continuously reaching out for more, we must begin to look within—within our regions, our communities, our homes, and ourselves—for ways to meet our needs while respecting water's life-sustaining functions. . . . The challenge now is to put as much human ingenuity into learning to live in balance with water as we have put into controlling and manipulating it.

1 CHAPTER

How Should the Water Supply Be Managed?

Chapter Preface

If viewing the earth from space, one would think that water is in endless supply. With three-fourths of the planet's surface covered by water, it is difficult to imagine humanity running out of this precious resource.

Yet the truth of the matter is that many places experience a shortage of usable water. In the Middle East, the western American states, and central Africa, for example, water is often a scarce commodity. The natural aridity of some regions, pollution of existing water sources, and overpopulation are the major factors that contribute to water shortages.

Attempts to solve water shortages focus either on finding new supplies of usable water or conserving existing sources. Building dams to collect water in reservoirs and drawing water from underground sites are two methods commonly used to increase the supply of available water. These methods, however, can cause environmental problems. For example, the construction of dams can disrupt the natural habitat of many species of wildlife. Such problems have led scientists to explore other possibilities, which range from the bizarre (floating icebergs to Los Angeles) to the mundane (collecting rainwater in cisterns).

The viewpoints in the following chapter present differing opinions on what causes water shortages and how to better manage the water supply so that all who need water—farmers, factories, and cities—have access to it.

"Water marketing can provide a mechanism for improving efficiency and environmental quality. "

Employ Market Incentives

Terry L. Anderson and Donald R. Leal

The U.S. federal government plays an important role in determining how America's water should be allocated. Some economists and others, however, believe that the free market can better determine who should own the rights to the nation's water resources. In the following viewpoint, excerpted from their book *Free Market Environmentalism*, Terry L. Anderson and Donald R. Leal maintain that free market incentives would allow those who need water to buy and sell water rights just as they would any other product. This would benefit both the economy and the environment, and would result in a fairer and more efficient allocation of water. Anderson is a professor of economics at Montana State University in Bozeman and a senior economist at the Pacific Research Institute public policy think tank in San Francisco. Leal is a research associate at the institute.

As you read, consider the following questions:

1. Why are well-specified water rights important, in the authors' opinion?
2. Why are structural solutions such as dams and reservoirs no longer popular solutions to water allocation, according to Anderson and Leal?
3. What do the authors believe is the primary reason for the change in how water is allocated in America?

Reprinted from: *Free Market Environmentalism* by Terry L. Anderson and Donald R. Leal, 1991, by permission of Westview Press, Boulder, Colorado.

Many people see free markets and the environment as incompatible; for them, the very notion of free market environmentalism is an oxymoron. Even many "free marketeers" find themselves on opposite sides of the fence when it comes to governmental regulation of the environment. Some will hold fast to the conviction that markets work best to allocate most of the goods and services we enjoy, but they will also argue that the environment is different and is too precious to be allocated on the basis of profits. . . .

This viewpoint will challenge this common perception and offer an alternative way of thinking about environmental issues, markets, and political choice. This way of thinking does not always provide solutions; instead, it concentrates on how alternative processes link information about the environment with individual incentives to interact with it. Here, the environment and the market are inextricably connected in a positive rather than a negative way.

Property Rights Are Important

At the heart of free market environmentalism is a system of well-specified property rights to natural resources. Whether these rights are held by individuals, corporations, non-profit environmental groups, or communal groups, a discipline is imposed on resource users because the wealth of the owner of the property right is at stake if bad decisions are made. Of course, the further a decision maker is removed from this discipline—as he is when there is political control—the less likely it is that good resource stewardship will result. Moreover, if well-specified property rights are transferable, owners must not only consider their own values, they must also consider what others are willing to pay. . . .

Free market environmentalism emphasizes an important role for government in the enforcement of property rights. With clearly specified titles—obtained from land recording systems, strict liability rules, and adjudication of disputed property rights in courts—market processes can encourage good resource stewardship. It is when rights are unclear and not well enforced that over-exploitation occurs. . . .

Free market environmentalism emphasizes the importance of market processes in determining optimal amounts of resource use. Only when rights are well-defined, enforced, and transferable will self-interested individuals confront the trade-offs inherent in a world of scarcity. As entrepreneurs move to fill profit niches, prices will reflect the values we place on resources and the environment. Mistakes will be made, but in the process a niche will be opened and profit opportunities will attract resource managers with a better idea. Remember that even externalities offer profit niches to the environmental entrepreneur who can define and enforce property rights to the unowned resource and charge the free-riding user. In cases where definition and enforcement costs are insurmountable, political solutions may be called for. Unfortunately, however, those kinds of solutions often become entrenched and stand in the way of innovative market processes that promote fiscal responsibility, efficient resource use, and individual freedom. . . .

"Whiskey is for drinkin' and water is for fightin'," Mark Twain wrote. In the arid West, where water is the lifeblood of agriculture, this adage has become especially appropriate as municipal, industrial, and environmental demands for water have come into more conflict. Traditionally, growing demands have been met with structural solutions, such as the Central Arizona Project that cost billions of dollars to deliver water primarily to municipal users in Phoenix and Tucson. But fiscal and environmental reality is forcing westerners to recognize that the days of solving water problems with concrete and steel are over. Colorado Governor Richard D. Lamm described the change:

> When I was elected governor in 1974, the West had a well-established water system. . . . Bureau [of Reclamation] officials and local irrigation districts selected reservoir sites and determined water availability. With members of the western congressional delegation, they obtained project authorization and funding. Governors supported proposals, appearing before congressional committees to request new projects, and we participated in dam completion ceremonies.

> In 1986, the picture is quite different. The boom in western resources development has fizzled. . . . Congress . . . has to worry about how to cut spending, not which [water] projects to fund. . . . Farmers are trying to stay in business and are recognizing that their water is often worth more than their crops. Policy-makers recognize that the natural environment must be protected because it is a major economic asset in the region.

This political, social, and economic climate ushered in a new era in managing water resources in the West. In the face of efforts to curtail government spending and protect the environment, the customary and legal institutions that govern water allocation must foster the conservation and efficient allocation of existing supplies and take water's growing recreational and environmental value into account. These institutions evolved during an era when federal outlays to fund huge water projects made trade-offs unnecessary, however, and they are not up to the task.

The Political Allocation of Water

For most of the twentieth century, the federal government financed the construction and maintenance of water storage and delivery projects designed to make the western desert "bloom like a rose." The Bureau of Reclamation and the Army Corps of Engineers administer the use of the water from these projects, providing nearly 90 percent of it to agricultural users who pay only a fraction of what it costs to store and deliver it. The artificially low prices for federal water promote waste at a time when water supplies are coming under increasing stress from industrial, municipal, and environmental demands. And despite these demands, the political allocation of federal water has been unresponsive, with few transfers of water made to other uses. What we have learned from the stronghold that agricultural interests exert on federal water is that if water runs uphill to money, it gushes uphill to politics.

A Popular Notion

In the arid West, the idea of buying and selling water rights on the open market is becoming increasingly popular. Large volumes of water must be shifted from agricultural to municipal use if the West is to continue its population growth and economic development. Many planners feel that a free market in water will encourage such a shift. . . . Many economists, lawyers, and policymakers advocate trading water rights, which would help establish market prices and encourage water conservation. Going beyond theory, water marketing is now a fact in several states that already permit the sale and purchase of water rights. Western water law allows for purchase of water in one area to be used in another.

Andrew A. Dzurik, *Water Resources Planning*, 1990.

The 1980s, however, have seen a major change in water policy. Free market environmental principles have become a coalescing theme among environmentalists and fiscal conservatives who oppose water projects that are both uneconomical and environmentally destructive. This theme was instrumental in defeating the 1982 Peripheral Canal initiative, a project to divert northern California water to southern California. Opponents successfully convinced voters of the high costs of the project as well as the detrimental environmental effects of draining fresh water from the Sacramento delta. Following the initiative's defeat, Thomas Graff, general counsel for the California Environmental Defense Fund, asked: "Has all future water-project development been choked off by a new conservationist-conservative alliance . . . ?" The answer appears to be yes. During the 1980s, new, large-scale federal water projects have come to a virtual halt.

20

Water marketing can provide a basis for extending the alliance into the 1990s, by encouraging efficient use, discouraging detrimental environmental effects, and reducing the drain on government budgets. Equally important, water marketing can release the creative power of individuals in the marketplace, enabling water users to bring to bear specific knowledge to respond to growing scarcities. As economist Rodney Smith explained, with water marketing "a farmer can apply his firsthand knowledge of his land, local hydrology, irrigation technology, and relative profitability of alternative crops to decide how much water to apply and which crops to grow on his land."

Clearly Defined Water Rights Are Needed

As with all aspects of free market environmentalism, water marketing depends on well-specified water rights; that is, rights must be clearly defined, enforceable, and transferable. Clearly defined and enforced water rights reduce uncertainty and assure that the benefits of water are captured. Transferable rights force users to face the full cost of water, including its value in other uses. If alternative uses are more valuable, then current users have the incentive to reallocate scarce water by selling or leasing it. Unfortunately, well-specified water rights are conspicuously absent from the legal institutions that govern the use of the resource. Governmental restrictions produce uncertainty of ownership, stymie water transfers, and promote waste and inefficiency in water use.

By removing these governmental restrictions and adhering more closely to the prior appropriation doctrine, water marketing can provide a mechanism for improving efficiency and environmental quality. . . .

During the 1980s, the management of water in the West entered a new era. Demands for limited water supplies, environmental concerns, the federal debt, and the incidence of legal conflicts over water have all increased, and a troubled farm economy was cursed with over-production. By far, the biggest impetus for change in water institutions has been the increase in environmental and recreational demand. As Environmental Defense Fund economist Zach Willey put it, "We've had 100 years of [water] development, and the environment's been kicked around pretty bad." But trying to rehabilitate the environment means recognizing all water interests. Willey concluded: "You're not going to do it by wholesale taking away of resources from industry and farmers. . . . You're going to do it through a system of incentives." Willey's approach is to "go out and make some deals," but before that can be accomplished institutional reforms are needed. The Bureau of Reclamation holds claim to 35 percent of the water delivered in the West, which is being supplied at highly subsidized prices. To make matters worse, trade that would transfer water to higher-valued alternatives is being stymied. Neither of those conditions is compatible with conservation or efficient allocation.

In order to reap the advantages of the market, policy makers must find ways to define property rights in water, enforce them, and make them transferable—and then guard against doctrines that erode these principles.

"The overexploitation of water resources continues to take place whether it is facilitated through construction projects or the marketing of water rights."

Market Incentives May Be Harmful

Helen Ingram

Helen Ingram is the author of numerous studies on water politics and is the acting director of the Udall Center for Studies in Public Policy at the University of Arizona in Tucson. In the following viewpoint, excerpted from her book *Water Politics: Continuity and Change*, she states that while market incentives can improve the allocation of water in the United States, they can also cause problems. Environmentalists and the rural poor are among those who Ingram believes would be harmed by allowing the nation's water to be allocated according to free market principles.

As you read, consider the following questions:

1. Why did environmentalists initially support water reallocation through market incentives, in Ingram's opinion?
2. How have courts supported the idea that water rights can be privately owned, according to the author?
3. Why does Ingram believe Indian tribes would be harmed if water was allocated solely on the basis of market incentives?

Reprinted from Helen Ingram, *Water Politics: Continuity and Change*, with permission of the University of New Mexico Press, © 1990 by the University of New Mexico Press.

In 1973, University of Arizona scholars Maurice M. Kelso, William E. Martin, and Lawrence Mack advised Arizonans that the answers to water scarcity lay not in the development of new supplies, but in the transfer of existing supplies to higher value uses. . . . A number of factors are responsible for the emergence of the new marketing era. . . .

Reallocation Leads to Efficiency

Reliance on marketing of water rights to determine water distributions satisfies water policy critics who wish for greater efficiency in allocation. Federal water development projects were vulnerable to the charge of being poor investments. In contrast, water reallocation could be rationalized as leading to greater efficiency. Even environmentalists were impressed by this argument when it was realized that reallocation was an alternative to dams. Certain so-called efficiency measures could stretch existing supplies and were much more cost effective than big capital development projects. The Berkeley office of the Environmental Defense Fund became one of the foremost advocates of the economic approach. A proposal whereby water conservation works in the Imperial Irrigation District could be funded by the metropolitan water department in exchange for the salvaged water was strongly put forward by these environmentalists.

The judiciary has reinforced the approval of the marketplace as an appropriate arena for water allocation. In *Sporhase v. Nebraska* in 1982, the United States Supreme Court declared that water was a commodity subject to interstate commerce clause scrutiny and that public ownership of water asserted by most western state statutes and constitutions was a legal fiction. There can be little doubt that the attitude of the court provided a strong impetus for rural-to-urban water transfers. The Sporhase case set an important precedent for the city of El Paso's attempt to secure water rights in the lower Rio Grande in New Mexico, arguing that the efforts of the agriculturalists in the area to protect their water and rural lifestyle was economic protectionism.

The transaction or decision-making costs in water transfers are low relative to the political water development process. Instead of the byzantine process of building support for federal water resources development made even more torturous later by elaboration of regulations, market exchanges required only a willing buyer and seller and a showing of nonimpairment of protected interests. Courts defend third-party interests in water transfers, but nothing like the full range of protections for the environment and broader social goals that operated in federal water development. Expansion of new or augmented water uses can take place throughout the market without going through an environmental impact statement or the test of value preferences that consent building for legislation involved. The mechanism of water marketing skirts the threat of federal reserved water rights, particularly as they apply to Indian tribes. If marketing can be extended sufficiently, it is conceivable that tribal rights could be bought out. In any case, the shutdown in the pipeline of federal money for projects has meant that tribes will have little public money to develop their water if they choose not to sell.

Transfers are not without opposition, and a number of political and legal roadblocks have kept the exchange of water through markets to a rather modest pace. Objections have been raised in Congress to allowing farmers to reap profits from selling water developed at subsidized costs for reclamation purposes. Even in those cases where Indian tribes are in favor of the lease or sale of water for off-reservation use, waivers to the Non-Intercourse Act are considerably difficult to obtain. State legislatures have debated and sometimes adopted laws regulating the rural-to-urban transfer of water. Some agricultural entities, like the Elephant Butte Irrigation District, have used their political and legal power to delay and undermine water transfers. Despite these impediments, however, few doubt that markets are to become the future forum for water exchange.

Losers in Contemporary Politics of Water

The apologists for water marketing typically argue that the losers are either nonexistent or few, and that they generally deserve their fate. Market discipline has a therapeutic effect. When markets work properly, there is a willing buyer and a wiling seller, and the supposed result is that both are better off. Presumably potential sellers are free to simply refuse to sell and avoid any perceived losses. Society also benefits by the transaction since resources are reallocated to the higher value use. The shift away from the federal purse eliminates the free riders or rent seekers who gain benefits without paying, as well as the wasteful bureaucracy serving narrow clientele. The most salient characteristic of the political perceptions about the distributive pattern of politics prevailing during the development era . . . was that there were only winners and no losers. Yet, as Theodore J. Lowi points out, all policies are redistributive in the long run, helping some at the expense of others. And, as discussed above, this was the case in the era of big federal projects. Similarly, contemporary market-oriented patterns of politics favor some interests over others. . . . [The losers include:]

25

1. *Environmentalists.* Environmentalist gains must be weighed against significant losses that are as yet not well recognized by spokespersons for the movement. The institutional mechanisms for managing water effectively are deteriorating. States and localities lack the jurisdiction or interest to adopt systemic or river basin perspectives on water management. Municipal water managers place a higher priority upon assured water supply than upon the social and ecological dislocations that may result from their market transactions. Because water rights or their priority are moved rather than wet water, it is often difficult to evaluate and mobilize to protect against adverse impacts of transfers. The natural limit which aridity imposes upon ecology is disregarded by human residents in the West as much as or more than in the past.

"The Government is pleased to announce there are no more environmental problems. The environment has all been sold to private developers."

Further, environmentalists have lost an important handle on growth in arid regions. A vast reservoir of water previously used by agriculture is now available. Lack of water is therefore not a good argument for defeating energy development projects.

Water shortage does not provide a credible argument to limit population expansion in most western cities as access to new supplies is gained through the water markets. Moving water from farms and rural areas has become legitimate even though the resulting use of water is much more environmentally damaging. To substitute housing developments with attendant problems of cars and air pollution, garbage disposal, and water pollution for cotton fields with fertilizers, pesticides, and water pollution, may not be such an excellent environmental bargain. Large populations in arid regions may have less flexibility in adjusting to the inevitable periodic droughts or to the long-term climate change that some scientists predict. Adverse environmental impacts also take place in areas of origin in water transfers. Retired farmland, especially if it has been laser leveled, only very slowly recovers natural vegetation. Blowing dust and tumbleweeds on fallow lands in the Avra Valley area in Arizona, bought by the city of Tucson for water rights, are illustrative.

Market Forums

Environmentalists have limited access to the market forums where water reallocation decisions occur. Environmental groups succeeded in putting in place procedural protections that would insure that environmental values be taken into account in federal water policy, but now this machinery affords little protection. Third-party and more general social interests are poorly represented by buyers and sellers in market transactions. States have begun to institute public welfare criteria allowing government to intervene in sales, leases, and transfers when broad social interests are at stake, but this legislative activity is in the early stages.

2. *The Disadvantaged.* Disadvantaged people including Indians and other rural minorities continue to lose in water decisions. Without question the extent of participation of disadvantaged people in water politics has grown. Instead of being left out of negotiations on water projects, the supposed benefits to Indian people and tribal support have rescued several projects from near certain defeat as the Central Arizona and Animas-La Plata projects experience illustrates. There is a difference, however, between gaining a place at the bargaining table and being able to control the substance or direction of the bargains being struck. Disadvantaged people have won something through a number of contemporary water developments, but that something is often quite remote from what they really wanted. Moreover, just as they were beginning to succeed, the water game changed. After dedicating many of their brightest young members to training in the law and winning greater security of water rights through the courts, the federal construction pro-

gram began winding down. Poor people no longer have much opportunity to develop their water resources with federal help. What construction money is available is overlaid with financing and evaluation requirements much stricter than those applied to development projects in the past.

Poor rural people are unlikely to profit from water sales because much of their attachment to the resource is noneconomic. Loss of water represents a sacrifice of opportunity, security, and self-determination. Research indicates that the predominant opinion in many rural communities is against sales, leases, and transfers of water. Rural respondents reflect a conviction that while a few individuals may be willing to sell and may profit thereby, the community as a whole will be worse off.

3. *Federal Agencies*. Federal construction agencies have doubtless lost ground in the current pattern of politics. The author of a most critical book published in the 1950s on the Army Corps of Engineers observes the present corps as a pale image of its former self. Power began to be shifted away from the agency with the establishment of the position of assistant secretary of the army for civil works in 1970 and has continued since.

The Bureau of Reclamation has been even more devastated. A reorganization of the bureau considered in 1987 would have at first moved the commissioner from the centers of power in Washington to Denver, an unlikely proposal in the 1960s era of [Commissioner] Floyd Dominy.

To some extent state and local water agencies have benefited from the diminution of federal authority. Water policy making is a good deal more decentralized than previously. This shift has had its price, however. Some state agencies are weak and lack the means to manage water resources effectively, especially when this entails regulating powerful local interests. State interests often conflict when it comes to management of river basins which cross state lines. . . .

Winners Still Win, Losers Still Lose

The outcome of water policy in terms of winners and losers has changed only slightly in the past twenty years. Development-oriented local elites were the main beneficiaries of the federal water development era. These interests continue to be the winners in prevailing patterns of water decisions. The previous losers, especially environmentalists, Indians, and poor rural people, while more influential than previously, continue to lose. For environmentalists there are some positive tradeoffs involved in the demise of big federal projects, but environmentally damaging water decisions continue. Indians have gained a place at the bargaining table, but the prizes they win are sometimes far from what they really want. Other interests that used to do better now fare poorly, including rural economies dependent on irrigated agriculture, and federal construction agencies. Further, the likelihood that a fundamental reshuffling of winners and losers will take place appears increasingly remote. With little unappropriated water remaining in the West, with ground water levels falling in a large number of river basins, and with ground- and surface water quality experiencing degradation, little flexibility remains to serve previously neglected interests without encountering entrenched opposition. . . .

The capacity of dominant interests to pursue advantages despite changes in decision making appears to be large. The overriding forces in water policy may be the nature and perceptions of the issue, and the political influence, resources, and skill of the local growth-oriented interests. The overexploitation of water resources continues to take place whether it is facilitated through construction projects or the marketing of water rights to users remote from the areas in which water naturally occurs. Until aridity is accepted as a natural limit to which humans must adapt their expectations and institutions, water resource decisions will continue to pay insufficient attention to impacts on the environment and the social and cultural values associated with this fundamental resource.

*"Small-scale actions . . . can promote
conservation of this precious resource."*

Conservation Is Necessary

Umberto Colombo

Often during droughts, citizens are urged to conserve water by
not watering lawns or washing cars, among other measures. In
the following viewpoint, Umberto Colombo agrees that conservation of water by individuals, governments, and industries can
help ensure that there is enough water to serve everyone's
needs. Colombo is director-general of the Agency for New
Technologies, Energy, and the Environment in Rome and the
president of the European Science Foundation.

As you read, consider the following questions:

1. Why does Colombo believe the world's water shortage
   problem will only worsen?
2. Why is water availability particularly a problem in Africa,
   according to the author?
3. How can individuals reduce their household water
   consumption, according to Colombo?

Water is an essential "common good" that until fairly recently was thought to be superabundant, and therefore used wastefully, especially in the wealthy industrialized nations.

But in reality water is a relatively scarce resource: extremely scarce in some parts of the world. And as the world's population grows and its standard of living gradually rises, the demand for water, and therefore its cost, is bound to increase.

Taking into account possible climate changes, the already-difficult water problem can only get more complicated. Since every increase of 1 degree centigrade in average temperature moves the temperate latitudes 100 or 200 kilometers (62 to 125 miles) farther away from the equator, the areas where farm productivity is now highest could eventually become semiarid or arid, with drastic consequences for world food production.

Promoting Conservation

Of course, large-scale projects will always be needed to transport fresh water from places where it abounds to places where it does not. In addition, cost-effective ways must be found to exploit new water resources: by desalinating seawater, for instance, and purifying polluted water. But more to the point are small-scale actions that, with relatively small investment, can promote conservation of this precious resource.

Sound water management starts with land-use and watershed management. Drainage must be designed to collect runoff, especially from torrential rains that lead to erosion and landslides. The creation of adequate vegetation cover, irrigation systems, and small interlinking ponds makes it possible to store water against dry seasons and prevent erosion.

Another aspect is the modernization of water treatment, recycling wherever possible and always aiming to prevent waste. Cascade use must be properly managed: in geographical terms, from higher to lower localities; in pollution terms, from lesser to more contaminating uses; in terms of priorities, taking adequate account of each country's typical needs, from domestic uses to farming, power generation, and industry.

A "Software" Approach

Accordingly, water-management strategies need to take a "software" approach, emphasizing the intangible and system organization. This implies a complex process made up of many different steps, relatively inexpensive and simple enough in themselves, but conceived as parts of a whole system and implemented from the bottom up. Naturally, large projects and costly solutions will still be needed where "soft" actions do not suffice.

Today, agriculture accounts for around two-thirds of all the water consumed worldwide. With the population growing steadily, it would be unthinkable to try to limit world food production or farm productivity. Irrigation, together with fertilizers and pesticides, is the principal means of increasing farm productivity, and in the past few decades it has been instrumental in fighting hunger in the third world, especially in Asia.

In 1900, 40 million hectares (99 million acres) of the world's farmlands were irrigated. By 1950 the figure had grown to 95 million hectares (235 million acres); by 1980 it was more than 200 million (494 million acres). During the 1980s the expansion of irrigation slowed, in some cases because of the appearance of symptoms of aquifer depletion, and in others due to the shelving of new irrigation projects that lost out to industry and cities in the growing competition for scarce water resources.

U.S. Average Indoor Water Use

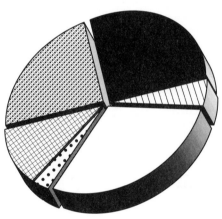

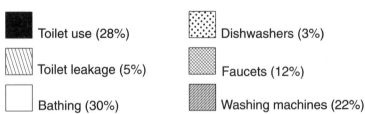

Source: Peter Drukmeir, *Earth Day 1990 Water Conservation Fact Sheet.*

Water availability is a particularly dramatic problem in many parts of Africa, where the combination of an arid climate, drought, soil depletion, and deforestation has aggravated the malnutrition of an exploding population. Here, as elsewhere, the problem must be thought through in new terms that take account of the complex interaction among the factors of food, water, land conservation, and preservation of genetic diversity.

Irrigation systems can be redesigned to give plants exactly the amount of water they need, without flooding the ground. The ultimate technology today consists of computerized drip irrigation, using underground humidity detectors to reduce water inputs to the minimum required for optimal production.

Plant geneticists are developing less-water-demanding crop strains; for instance, rice cultivars that need not be submerged in water (though it acts as a thermostat against excessive cold and heat). Plants that tolerate brackish water are also beng developed, though in this case one should contemplate crop rotation, which is essential to prevent soil depletion.

Other important aspects are the replacement of chemical pesticides with biological pest-control techniques, and the application of fertilizer directly to plant roots, which reduces water pollution and the oxygen-starvation of lakes.

Saving Water in Industry

Industrial water requirements can also be rationalized. Enormous amounts are consumed, and heavily polluted, by paper mills, tanneries, and many processes in the chemical, textile, and hydrometallurgical industries. But it is proving increasingly feasible to design solutions that require much less water. Now paper mills, textile factories, and tanneries consume many times less water, and contaminate it less, than even their very-recent predecessors.

The two fundamental aspects which should be provided for in all industrial activities are the purification of waste water to make it suitable for other uses (the quality of treated water is determined to a great extent by purification costs) and the creation of closed cycles, whereby waste water is recycled in the industrial process itself. In this connection, many suggestions can be gleaned by studying the membranes and biochemical processes that purify and regulate water flow in living organisms, including human beings.

Lastly, numerous steps can be taken to rationalize our household and sanitary uses of water, for instance by installing alternate-action toilet tanks, or water taps that turn on only when a person's hands are underneath them. The main issue is to educate the public and adopt water-conservation policies; that is, "soft" steps that can also work through the market by turning water into a long-term strategic factor.

The price of water must increasingly reflect its scarcity and the real costs of its supply. Higher rates may be more acceptable if part of the increase is used to pay for investments aimed at limiting consumption.

In conclusion, important opportunities are opening up for wide-ranging actions that require no earthshaking decisions or mammoth investments, but that comprise an organized and integrated package of often-intangible initiatives that involve participation by individual citizens. This is a promising path that should guide future strategies for managing water resources.

"Conservation or preservation of water resources will not make us better able to manage water problems."

Conservation Is Ineffective

David Lewis Feldman

In the following viewpoint, David Lewis Feldman argues that conservation is not an effective way of managing the water supply. The word "conservation," he maintains, has different meanings to different people. Therefore, it is difficult to implement conservation policies that are effective. Feldman is a staff member in the energy division of the Oak Ridge National Laboratory, one of the U.S. Department of Energy's national research and development laboratories. He is the author of *Water Resources Management: In Search of an Environmental Ethic*, from which this viewpoint is excerpted.

As you read, consider the following questions:

1. Why does the United States have a water crisis, in Feldman's opinion?
2. How does the author distinguish between *preservation* and *conservation*?
3. What four reasons does Feldman give for his belief that conservation will not help Americans manage the nation's water supply?

Reprinted from David Lewis Feldman, *Water Resources Management: In Search of an Environmental Ethic*, 1991, with permission of the Johns Hopkins University Press, © 1991 by The Johns Hopkins University Press.

Water problems are the result of misguided and misdirected human choices. They are not the product of physical or technical limitations of the resource itself. All the fresh water there ever was still exists on this earth. Overdevelopment of arid regions, pollution, and failure to plan for drought have made water resources unavailable in particular places and at particular times. Failure to appreciate the implications of this simple fact has directly contributed to an impending water crisis in the United States. In short, regional, national, and local disputes over water stem from the way political, legal, and social institutions manage.

Our current water crisis revolves around demand exceeding supply—especially in the generally arid but rapidly growing Far West—and the quality of available supply becoming diminished nationwide by pollution. In the latter instance, nonpoint contamination of water caused by agriculture and storm water runoff is inadequately encompassed by current regulatory policy. In some instances, air pollution through acid precipitation damages lakes and streams, making the burning of coal a key source of water pollution. Moreover, demand and quality concerns extend equally to ground and surface waters and are compounded by the relative absence of a national policy for the former. Studies of these issues suggest the need to rethink our basic attitudes about water as a commodity to be exploited for individual gratification with little regard for the consequences of our actions.

In order to meet the challenges of this crisis, we must first understand that natural resources policy in the United States has been based upon values that maximize short-term exploitive gain and minimize equity. These values have encouraged practices that impose negative environmental impacts upon water and related land resources. They have also discouraged alternative solutions to water problems that are less costly and potentially more beneficial to society as a whole. Thus, in order to address these problems, a way must be found to encompass values that maximize long-term social benefit in water resources policy. . . .

Conservation and Preservation

In recent years, critics of water policy have focused on the need for policies to encourage prudent use of water and to minimize practices that pollute and deplete it. Many of these critics are merely reviving an older approach to the management of water resources, an approach labeled *conservation*. This older approach was frequently invoked during the nineteenth century, when many of the fiercest water resources battles were raging in places such as California's Owens Valley and Tuolumne

36

River. Unfortunately, the term *conservation* ranges in meaning from the exploitation of nature on behalf of efficiency to a humble acknowledgement of our moral limits as members of an intricate, natural web.

"WE KNOW YOU'RE IN THERE, LADY—WE'VE GOT YOUR AZALEAS SURROUNDED!... GIVE UP THE WATER SPRINKLER AND NOBODY GETS HURT!"

By permission of Doug Marlette and Creators Syndicate.

Conservation properly refers to the management of natural resources in such a way as to assure the production of maximum sustainable yields for present and future generations. As defined by proponents of scientific resource management such as Gifford Pinchot (1865-1946), conserving a resource means maximizing its efficient use while minimizing the transaction costs entailed in its management. This is accomplished by limiting exploitation to a level sustainable by the resource's natural processes of recuperation.

Preservationists, on the other hand, assert that the exploitation of nature ought to be guided by a value system that transcends instrumental human needs. John Muir (1838-1914), arguably the best known early American preservationist, defined appropriate exploitation, especially of water, in sacred, almost religious terms. Muir suggested that his personal campaign to prevent the damming of the Tuolumne River in Yosemite Valley, California, was rooted in aesthetic truths impermeable to scientific scrutiny and only understandable to the heart.

More recently, philosophers such as Tom Regan and Paul Taylor have defended preservation on Kantian grounds. They suggest that all living things, including flora and fauna, should

37

be treated as ends in themselves and have rights that should not be violated for short-term human gain. According to the preservationist ethic, the principal criterion of a natural resources policy should be the protection of noneconomic values (the beauty of a free-flowing, white-water river, for example). It also implies that the concept of equity should embrace relationships among all living things, not just people. A preservationist would contend that allocation of water should be based on the needs of flora and fauna in both the region from which the water is being transferred and the region to which it is being delivered. Water laws should encompass the minimal water needs of plants, animals, and people. A serious problem with this contention is the difficulty in attributing to plants and animals the same rights we attribute to people, since flora and fauna are unable to advance their own claims against society.

Both bases for preservation point to the need to consider the process of natural ecosystems apart from calculations of economic efficiency. Thus, both are consistent with public choice views, which suggest that those who manage water resources should seek conformity between the political and natural worlds.

Why Conservation Is Ineffective

At this point, it is necessary to consider why a shift from development to conservation or preservation of water resources will not make us better able to manage water problems. First, the meaning of *conservation* is ambiguous, shifting, and often elusive. Second, both conservation and preservation have been depicted by their proponents in a fashion far too romantic and emotional to guide practical policy. Third, the question of what instruments are optimal for carrying out the objectives of conservation or development must still be answered. Fourth, prior to selecting such instruments, the necessity for government intervention must be established.

Conservation and preservation differ in their degree of optimism regarding the sustainability of nature in the face of human impacts. Conservation values water as an extrinsic commodity, preservation thinks of it as having intrinsic value. This contrast underscores the role of rational fallibility in defending public policies toward nature.

It is important that agreement over the value of water be established before institutional arrangements are developed, or policy instruments inappropriate to long-term management goals may be inadvertently selected. While this may be excusable in some situations, it is less justifiable in a developed polity, which has the bureaucratic ability and political will to make long-term decisions.

"Much western water is used on water-consumptive, low-value crops."

Force Agriculture to Use Less Water

Marc Reisner

A large amount of water is used to grow crops, especially in California and other western U.S. states. Marc Reisner in the following viewpoint asserts that farmers waste valuable water on crops such as rice and alfalfa instead of planting crops that require less water. He believes that cities, industries, and the environment will all benefit if agricultural water use is sharply reduced. Reisner is the author of *Cadillac Desert*, a history of water and the American West.

As you read, consider the following questions:

1. Why do California farmers grow crops that require an excessive amount of water, according to Reisner?
2. Some experts believe that cutting water to agriculture will increase food prices and cause food shortages. Why does Reisner disagree with this theory?
3. What does the author mean when he says that water development has attained "the status of a secular religion in the American West"?

Reprinted, with permission, from Marc Reisner, "The Next Water War: Cities Versus Agriculture," *Issues in Science and Technology*, vol. 4, no. 2 (1989). Copyright 1989 by the National Academy of Sciences, Washington, D.C.

Like most Easterners, when I first came to California I was unprepared for the reality that it was so dry. On television and in the movies, the state had always looked lush and green. But as I drove across it, California—along with so much of the West—seemed far more arid than the mind's-eye image I had formed. It was a revelation to see just how much of this continent the desert owns.

Thus I supposed that the water problems of the West—with limited supplies of this precious resource stretched thin by burgeoning growth in population and industrial activity—were serious indeed. I was wrong. The fact is that the region has plenty of water for any rational need. Our problem is one of management. What we have in the American West is a stupefyingly inefficient—almost Soviet-style—system of water management and allocation. With relatively few adjustments—which may, I admit, require some real political courage to bring about—there would be plenty of water for further economic growth. And there would be water to repair some of the environmental damage that has already occurred—to bird habitats in the rivers and dried-up wetlands of the Pacific flyway, for example, and to estuarine treasures, such as San Francisco Bay, that produce so much aquatic life.

Taking a Lot, Returning a Little

To truly understand the use—and misuse—of water in the West, one must take a cold, detached look at agriculture.

In California, where I live, agriculture accounts for 85 percent of all water use, nearly all of it for irrigation; that figure is even higher in most other western states. But agriculture accounts for only 2.5 percent of the California economy. And, although the state economy has grown by $200 billion over the past 16 years (to $550 billion), agriculture's contribution has remained static at $14 billion.

Even in New Mexico, the least urbanized western state, agriculture returns just about 18 percent of the state's income—but uses 92 percent of the water.

What does all that water grow? In California, the number-one crop in terms of water consumption is irrigated pasture—grass and hay for cows and sheep—which used approximately 5.3 million acre-feet in 1986. This was equal to the amount of water consumed by all 27 million people in the state, and that includes swimming pools and watered lawns. And what was irrigated pasture *worth* to California? An invisible $94 million in gross receipts, representing about one five-thousandth of the economy. But it used one-seventh of the water on which that munificent economy depends.

Consider alfalfa, the second most water-consumptive crop. In

1986, irrigating alfalfa required as much water—3.9 million acre-feet—as metropolitan Los Angeles and the Bay Area combined. Drinking water, toilets, lawns, gardens, showers, swimming pools, car washes—everything. What did alfalfa return? About $630 million. Even when you add secondary benefits, alfalfa generated less economic activity than a few square blocks of downtown L.A.

Cotton and Rice

Now we come to cotton, the third most water-consumptive crop. The San Joaquin Valley's million acres of cotton require around 3 million acre-feet of water per year. That's water for 15 million people—or 15 times the population of Nevada. In 1986, cotton added $842 million to the California economy. Better than alfalfa and grass, but still not much to brag about.

No More Gardens in the Desert

The rice paddies and alfalfa fields of California's Central Valley aren't officially among the seven wonders of the modern world, but they certainly qualify as a miracle.

Stretching out as far as the eye can see in the desert east of San Francisco, the soggy expanses defy nature, yielding several million pounds a year of the most water-intensive crops known to man. Even as the rest of the state lies parched from seven years virtually without rain, drought is just another word in this small corner of paradise.

But the flowing waters here are no act of God. They are an act of Congress, drawn up 50 years ago to promote agricultural development. . . .

But that well ran dry when President Bush reluctantly signed into law a dramatic shift in the way water is allocated in California. Soon, urban areas, wetlands and businesses may have enough water to thrive. And agribusiness, which uses 80% of the water in the state but contributes less than 5% of its gross domestic product, will have to abandon its vision of a moist Eden in the desert sand.

Nancy Hass, *Financial World*, January 5, 1993.

Rice is the fourth most water-consumptive crop in California. Rice, you could say, is not everyone's idea of an appropriate desert crop, since it grows only in manmade lakes. The main reason it is grown at all in California is because many of our rice farmers buy water from the Bureau of Reclamation at fabulously subsidized prices (as do many of the cotton, alfalfa, and hay farmers). But rice used much more water than the whole Bay Area in 1986—enough for 10 million people. Its gross value was a pitiful $204 million.

Suppose the cotton, alfalfa, pasture, and rice acreage in California was entirely eliminated? Suppose further that the land was not replanted with more sensible crops—truly a worst-case scenario, since you can grow practically anything in California. The agricultural industry would decline, from $14 billion to $12.3 billion a year in gross revenue, but there would instantly be enough water for 70 million more Californians . . . God forbid. That $1.7 billion loss of revenue, by the way, is exactly the cost of the proposed Auburn Dam that farmers want taxpayers to build for them. By simply retiring the land we'd get 75 times more water for our money.

Use It or Lose It

How has it come to this? How is it that in the western states—which are for the most part semiarid or arid, which have been experiencing tremendous population growth, and which have become dramatically more urbanized and industrialized since World War II—we allow a few extremely low-value forage and fodder crops to claim 50, 60, even 80 percent of the water?

There's no simple answer—is there ever a simple answer?—only a curious admixture of weather, confining legal doctrine, stubborn old habit, bureaucratic self-interest, socialist economics, and religion.

During the nineteenth century—when early western water rights were established—the American West was like a separate continent, isolated from the rest of the country by enormous distances, a primitive transportation system, and a ferocious and impetuous climate. Our forebears in the West felt an urgent need to be self-sufficient in food production. You couldn't easily import beef from Iowa or Texas, as you can today. So a lot of early and senior water rights were very large, based on the need to raise enormous forage acreage for cattle. The people who held these water rights—and who passed them on to their descendants—often formed irrigation districts that built canals and dams that are by now fully amortized. Therefore those who inherited these early water rights often owned a great volume of very inexpensive water.

When the Bureau of Reclamation came along in 1902, it offered cheap water to thousands of other farmers throughout the West, who were—and remain—exempted from paying interest on the taxpayers' investment in expensive aqueducts and dams. Imagine a $200,000 house, payable over 40 years with no interest charged at all. Your payments would be $416 a month instead of $1600 to $1800 a month. That is the order-of-magnitude savings the bureau's privileged farmer-clients enjoy.

Cheaper than Dirt

In some locales, the bureau still sells water, legally or not—some think not—for less than half a cent per ton, literally cheaper than dirt. This is socialist water—it's hypocritical to call it anything else, even if it means undermining the image of the region's rugged-individualist yeoman farmer. When water costs $7.50 per acre-foot, it's cheaper to waste it than to conserve it. And we are talking here about one-third of the irrigation water currently used in the American West.

So here we have two reasons—one historic, the other economic—for low-value crops (and water waste and inefficiency) that fit hand-in-glove with a third reason: the doctrine of appropriative rights. This preeminent legal framework within which western water rights are acquired, held, and lost, can be boiled down to a fine essence of five words: *Use it or lose it*. Thus, if you were to shift from irrigated pasture to oranges, you could reduce your water consumption by two-thirds. In fact, you could substitute almost any crop for pasture and reduce your water consumption. But then, under appropriative rights doctrine, your neighbor could simply take the water you no longer use, unless you somehow arranged to sell it.

Too Much Food

What about that prospect of selling it? In the case of water that has been developed and is sold by the Bureau of Reclamation—enough water, in theory, for the domestic uses of the entire population of the United States—I have seen almost no water rights being transferred or sold. Although the bureau has been talking about a "new mission," about "redefining its goals," it seems to me that its major goal remains to supply cheap water for as long as possible. I've spoken in person with the Commissioner of Reclamation and both Assistant Commissioners, and none of them said that the bureau is going to help its client farmers sell or rent water rights on a large scale—even if they want to. And the bureau has no plans to raise water rates substantially, even where projects are foundering in debt.

One reason is that if the Bureau of Reclamation gets into the business of redistributing water, or selling more expensive—which is to say, more realistically priced—water, it knows it will never have to build another dam. If I were an engineer—the Bureau of Reclamation is full of engineers—I would want to build more dams.

There's still another reason why so much western water is used on water-consumptive, low-value crops such as pasture and alfalfa. Outside of California, Arizona, and the Northwest, the region's bitter, high-altitude climate doesn't really let you grow much of anything else.

And yet even in California, where the most valuable crop, by far, is grapes—California's grape industry is worth more than a billion and a half dollars per year, or 15 times the value of irrigated pasture—the grape acreage is barely half as large as the pasture acreage.

So why, even in mediterranean California, aren't we raising more grapes and fewer cows? Partly for the reasons mentioned above: If you have cheap water and a large water right, and western water law gives your neighbor any water you don't use, you might as well keep raising grass. To a western farmer, there is no terror like losing water rights. But another reason is this: The country doesn't *need* that much land to grow grapes. Or lettuce. Here we are in the age of the salad bar, and here is California growing the overwhelming share of the nation's lettuce, but this colossal lettuce crop needs just 168,000 acres. The avocado crop needs only 74,000 acres. The whole California lemon crop requires just 50,000 acres. With a relatively small amount of cropland devoted to it, California now grows a third of the table food in the United States.

It's not surprising, then, that I have to smile when someone accuses me of trying to doom us all to starvation by shifting water out of irrigation. The basic problem with U.S. agriculture is that we grow too much food! I have to smile, too, when some grower tells me that if the Bureau of Reclamation doubles or triples its water prices, then food prices will double or triple, too. That insults my intelligence. In California, we have farmers buying an acre-foot of federal water for $10 or $15, and other farmers buying State Water Project water for $50 an acre-foot, but they're both in business, and the one guy's tomatoes don't cost three times as much as the other's.

A Sense of Conquest

Let me add one last, speculative reason why I think water in the West seems to gravitate to the lowest rather than the highest economic uses. It's that water development, in my opinion, has long attained the status of a secular religion in the American West.

We say that we love the desert, those of us who live here. If that's true at all, it's only partially true. When you consider the passion and the money that we bring to the job of transforming the desert, you could easily conclude that we hate it. What we really want is a Miami (look at Beverly Hills) or an Illinois (look at the Sacramento Valley) where it doesn't rain. We may drive through the desert—in an air-conditioned car, of course—"experiencing" its grandeur. But we need to come home to a swimming pool and a big green lawn in the midst of that desert. We love to see those agricultural oases, those big swaths of green in the desert's vast austere emptiness. We tweak its majestic indifference by making it bloom.

Free Water for Farmers

For too long, huge corporate farms have been able to skirt Federal limits on low-cost, taxpayer-subsidized water. For too long, agricultural corporations have gotten away with "double dipping" on both crop and water subsidies. . . .

Domestic users can limit toilet-flushing and lawn-watering all they want, but the fact is that conservation steps are of little consequence. There is a veritable tidal wave of water allocated to agriculture—to the detriment of other important needs.

Redding Record & Searchlight, 1991.

And where we have rescued land from the desert's possession, we don't want to give it up. We don't want the desert to reclaim what we have stolen from it at such enormous effort and expense. Seeing those alfalfa fields growing around Reno, or crossing the Tehachapis and heading up the San Joaquin Valley and seeing that sudden explosion of green, gives us not just a sense of conquest—of accomplishment—but also a peace of mind. After all, when you come right down to it, the desert is the most frightening landscape on earth.

That peace of mind—the stability—offered by irrigated agriculture had great economic and social value a hundred years ago. It represented deliverance from the cyclical agonies of boom and bust. But local economies have markedly changed. Nevada, for example, had the good sense to cultivate the four most stable industries on earth: gambling, prostitution, marriage, and divorce. And the economic importance of recreation, retirement, and high technology throughout the region is vastly out of proportion to irrigated grass and alfalfa. But these crops enjoy a certain unordained priority, as if this were . . . 1894.

In Colorado, the alfalfa crop uses 27 percent of the state's water and contributes a measly $160 million to the state's economy. Tourism takes a tiny fraction of that water but contributes $2 billion or $3 billion to Colorado's economy. Tourists prefer their water in roaring mountain streams, not on boring alfalfa fields. In California, the water in the South Fork of the American River is worth much more *in* the river than taken out for irrigation: The whitewater rafting business on the South Fork pumps several million dollars into Placer County's economy each year. Because there are no water development costs, that river represents pure profits. But the South Fork is scheduled to be dammed and diverted, because of that religious, uncompromising desire to keep the desert in bloom.

Toward Meaningful Change

Where does this leave us? Potentially with a war on our hands. True, the growers now own most of the water rights. But I don't know when westerners ever signed a Magna Carta proclaiming that agriculture has a God-given right to appropriate 85 to 90 percent of the region's water, for all time.

One day soon the urban voters of the West—who are the great majority today—are going to realize that agriculture—not Los Angeles, Las Vegas, or Phoenix—is the big *environmental* problem in the West, too. The blame for all the salmon rivers destroyed, the California wetlands acreage down to 5 percent of what it once was, millions of migratory waterfowl gone, the deer and elk and mountain sheep usurped from their traditional grazing lands, and the pesticides contaminating groundwater and Lake Mead and San Francisco Bay can't be laid at the cities' doors. And since something like 80 percent of all Californians and Nevadans now say they would side with nature in a contest with economic growth, this realization is going to count for a great deal when it finally hits home.

And people will someday realize, too, that they can have economic growth without ruining any more rivers and wetlands, and without building any more dams. They will start treating western water as the precious and scarce commodity that it is, and stop giving farmers oodles of subsidized water to grow subsidized crops.

"Renewing US leadership on desalination technology will yield untold benefits."

Desalinate Seawater

Paul Simon

Seawater cannot be consumed by humans because of its salt content. Today, however, desalination plants can remove the salt and thus make seawater into drinking water. In the following viewpoint, Paul Simon states that desalinated seawater could provide the world with much-needed water for consumption and industry. Simon, a democrat, is a U.S. senator from Illinois.

As you read, consider the following questions:

1. Why might water cause conflict between nations, according to Simon?
2. Why did the United States cut back on its desalination research, in the author's opinion?
3. Why does Simon believe Saudi Arabia and Israel are especially interested in desalination?

Paul Simon, "It's Time for a Breakthrough in Desalination," *The Christian Science Monitor*, March 26, 1991. Reprinted with permission.

Amid the massive coverage of the Gulf war and the lesser coverage of California's drought, an unfamiliar word began to enter the American lexicon: desalination—the process of extracting fresh water from sea water.

When Saddam Hussein resorted to oil spillage as a weapon of war, the public learned that Saudi Arabia relies on desalination plants for much of its fresh water. As California's drought has worsened, some are touting desalination as an option to assure adequate water supplies. And on our other coast, Florida is having its own water-supply problems.

Lack of fresh water increasingly is a brake on economic development and a source of friction between nations and between states and regions here at home. On a trip I made with Senate colleagues through the Middle East, both Israeli Prime Minister Yitzhak Shamir and Egyptian President Hosni Mubarak talked passionately of water needs.

A Source of Conflict

Just as today oil drives the energy engine for much of the industrialized world and thus causes international friction, tomorrow water will be a cause of intense competition and conflict as nations vie over a fundamental life-sustaining resource.

Saudi Arabia relies on desalination technologies that convert salt water to fresh water. Out of necessity, the Saudis have employed a technology that will become increasingly important in the future in the arid nations of the Middle East, but also in much of the rest of the world, including the United States.

Saudi Arabia can convert salt water to fresh water because the Saudis have the economic resources to afford using the present technologies. The US armed forces there did the same during the war, again because we could afford it.

But Egypt, with its mushrooming population, is able to use only 4 percent of its land, mostly along the Nile. And as its population grows, less and less of that land can be used to produce food. Egypt is right on the Mediterranean, with an abundance of water at hand—but water Egypt cannot afford to use because it doesn't have the money to use present desalination techniques.

Likewise, Mauritania is desperately poor in large part because of lack of water, yet it is right on the ocean. When I visited Mauritania a few years ago the people were growing only 10 percent of their own food. If the Mauritanians could use the water at their doorstep, they could dramatically improve their quality of life—and be food exporters.

According to a report by the Office of Technology Assessment, American industry was at the forefront of desalination technology throughout the 1960s and into the 1970s, thanks to

President Kennedy's special interest in the subject. Our efforts peaked in 1967, when federal funding reached $119 million in 1990 dollars.

Contracts Lost to Japanese, Europeans

Because today's process of distillation is energy-intensive, the oil crisis of the early 1970s brought a dramatic drop in interest and research. By the late 1980s, US-funded research had dwindled to a few hundred thousand dollars a year. When we ended most government sponsorship for desalination research during the early 1970s, Japanese and European firms, some of which were and still are government-supported, began securing contracts that earlier would have gone to American firms. . . .

Seawater to Drink

As drought continues to threaten many regions, seawater is becoming a reasonable solution to the dearth of potable water. Once an exotic process limited to desert settlements and expensive island developments, desalination now appeals even to large cities.

Pouring out 2 billion gallons a day worldwide, desalination plants currently supply the needs of high technology, oil refineries, and power plants. They also quench the thirst of entire communities. In Florida, which leads the United States in residential use, the largest of 110 desalination plants serves the city of Cape Coral, delivering 15 million gallons a day.

One reason for desalination's increasing popularity is the steady decline in the amount of fuel it requires, which is the main cost of the process. Modern techniques generate 100 units of water for every unit of energy consumed. Four decades ago, rudimentary distillation took 25 energy units to produce a unit of drinking water.

Roberta Friedman, *Technology Review*, August/September 1989.

I have introduced bipartisan legislation that would charter a long-term commitment for the US to reenter the desalination research field. . . .

Saudi Arabia and Israel are doing research. The Russians are interested because they have great arid lands. Interest is growing in California, the Southwest, and Florida.

The major technical obstacle at the moment is energy efficiency. State-of-the-art desalination technologies require enormous amounts of energy to create relatively modest amounts of potable water.

While this problem is not insurmountable for a cash-rich and energy-rich nation like Saudi Arabia, it keeps the technology out of reach for most nations facing dire water shortages.

One positive side effect of the tragic conflict in the Persian Gulf is that it might enable us to focus world resources and attention on the need to accelerate work on desalination technologies. We should seize the chance to make sure we are prepared to deal with the inevitable situation of massive and dire water shortages in many parts of the world.

This is an issue that could cause future wars if we do not vigorously pursue research. Renewing US leadership on desalination technology will yield untold benefits later, in strengthened prospects for peace in the Middle East, in economic security here at home, and in helping to end hunger around the world.

> *"Adequately treated sewage water can be reused as irrigation water for crops, forests and parks and to recharge ground-water deposits."*

Recycle Wastewater

Robert W. Adler and Trish Mace

While many regions have shortages of clean water, they have an abundance of wastewater. In the following viewpoint, Robert W. Adler and Trish Mace propose that sewage water be recycled for use in industry and agriculture. Adler is a senior attorney with the Natural Resources Defense Council in Washington, D.C. Mace is a scientist in the council's Los Angeles office. The NRDC is an environmental group that works to promote the wise use of natural resources.

As you read, consider the following questions:

1. Why is Southern California facing a severe water shortage, according to the authors?
2. How can some water contaminants actually be beneficial, according to Adler and Mace?
3. How does the United States compare to other nations in its use of reclaimed water, according to the authors?

Reprinted from Robert W. Adler and Trish Mace, "Water, Water, Everywhere a Shortage, Yes, but Who Should Conserve . . . and Why Do We Waste So Much?" *Los Angeles Times*, April 29, 1990. Reprinted with permission.

Los Angeles has two major water problems. The first is too little water. The second is too much water.

California's imminent water shortage by now is well known. . . . Residents are bracing for some strict water-saving measures—bans on using water to hose down driveways or sprinkle lawns and gardens, moratoriums on new connections and household rationing.

Then how can Los Angeles have too much water? Each year the city and county produce billions of gallons of sewage waste-water, most of which is partially treated then dumped into the Pacific. This effluent is a major source of coastal water pollution. Equally important, it is lost forever as a valuable source of recycled water.

The real problem, then, is finding a way to resolve this hydrologic paradox. Can the billions of gallons of sewage dumped into Southern California coastal waters be redirected to profitable use? And if this water is so polluted, is it safe to do so?

How Water Is Used

To answer these questions, some background is needed on water use in the region and methods of waste-water reclamation.

The serious water shortages facing Southern California should come as no surprise. After all, America's second-largest city sits in the middle of what is essentially a desert. What is surprising is that the problem has been postponed for so long.

For many years Southern Californians have been spoiled by ample water deliveries, despite rapid population growth and sparse local supplies. In 1952 the Metropolitan Water District issued the Laguna Declaration, which promised to supply Southern California with sufficient water to spur postwar economic growth. And it did so with a vengeance—water from the Colorado River, the Mono Lake basin, the High Sierra and the Owens Valley bathed Los Angeles despite steady population growth over the past half-century.

But now, many of Southern California's traditional outside water sources are drying up. Because of a court decision a quarter-century ago, California's share of the Colorado River is being reduced. Other litigation has cut water supplies from Mono Lake and the Owens Valley. Combined with below-average precipitation, the region now faces a severe shortage.

More important, the steady stream of low-priced water has given Southern Californians little incentive to use it efficiently. Americans in general treat water as a virtually unlimited resource, using almost 50% more water per capita than the nearest runner-up nation, and almost five times as much as some industrialized countries. But Southern California, because the area is hotter and drier than other regions, uses about twice as much water per person than is the case in New York or other Eastern states. And California is almost entirely dependent on irrigation to grow more than 200 crops.

Part of the solution to this problem lies in more efficient use of water. While conservation—such as installing toilets that use only 1.5 gallons per flush, as Los Angeles has mandated, and water-saving showerheads and faucets—can and should make a big difference, an equally valid aspect is why water rationing is imminent when billions of gallons of water are being dumped into the Pacific each year. Sixteen sewage-treatment plants from Santa Barbara to San Diego dump 1.3 billion gallons of waste-water every day into Southern California coastal waters.

Why can't this water be reused to help meet the region's freshwater needs? One reason is that this sewage—much of which receives only advanced primary treatment—carries with it massive amounts of pollution.

Recycling Facilities Being Built

California has some 200 water reclamation or recycling facilities and another 162 expected to come on line by 2000. An estimated 569,000 acre-feet of reclaimed water is expected to be in use in another decade, mostly in southern California.

Betty Brickson and Rita Schmidt Sudman, *Western Water*, September 1992.

Many of these pollutants can be removed with better treatment. While not clean enough to drink or use for other human-contact uses, adequately treated sewage water can be reused as irrigation water for crops, forests and parks and to recharge ground-water deposits. In some cases, pollutants that interfere with water reuse—especially metals and other toxics—come from industries that discharge their wastes into public sewage-treatment plants. These industries are legally required to "pre-treat" their wastes before they reach sewage plants; better pre-treatment and enforcement of existing standards would allow cleaner, reusable sewage effluent.

Some of the chemicals—such as nitrogen and phosphorus—seen as "contaminants" in sewage effluent are actually beneficial nutrients in irrigation water. Sewage reuse can improve agriculture, because nutrients are released slowly, rather than in a single large dose, as is the case with chemical fertilizers.

Waste-water reuse is not a new idea. There are more than 1,000 waste-water reuse projects in the United States in which water is reused for irrigation, industrial cooling and processing and ground-water recharge. In the Los Angeles area, about 30%

of the sewage water produced by the county—160 million gallons per day out of 530 million gallons—is treated in levels clean enough for reuse—irrigation of parks, aquifer recharge and industrial uses. These are noteworthy efforts. But less than half of this highly treated water (70 million out of 160 million gallons per day) is reused, with the remaining 90 million gallons discharged daily into the ocean.

The city of Los Angeles and other Southern California communities are even further behind in water-reuse programs, but there is some progress. San Diego, for example, is building a 1-million-gallon-per-day reclamation facility, to sell reclaimed water to area growers, local industries and Caltrans. Los Angeles has reclaimed water available in Griffith Park and the Sepulveda Basin.

Nationwide only about a fifth of 1% of water use in the United States is met by reclaimed water. By comparison, reclaimed water met 4% of Israel's total water needs in 1980, and is expected to reach 16% by the year 2000. Surely we can do much better, both in the Los Angeles region and in the nation as a whole. . . . The 90 million gallons of reusable water that Los Angeles County alone dumps into the Pacific each day could meet more than half the area's impending water shortage.

Transportation Costs

Distribution cost and the lack of adequate conveyance systems are the primary reasons why less than half of this waste water is reused. It is ironic that water transported hundreds of miles across the state, from Mono Lake and the Colorado River, has an economic advantage over water reclaimed in the county because of conveyance costs.

Recycled water should probably not be used for drinking water or other home consumption. But only a small fraction of total water use is in the home—in California, for example, nine out of every 10 gallons of fresh water are used for crop irrigation. Potable-quality water currently going to crop irrigation could be sent to Los Angeles for urban use, in return for nutrient-rich reclaimed sewage water for crop irrigation.

Much work needs to be done to determine the best ways to increase waste-water reuse in Southern California. What is abundantly clear, however, is that the region will no longer be able to turn to water from other areas to meet current water needs—much less any additional growth. At the same time, Los Angeles and environs can no longer afford to commit the dual sin of polluting Southern California's valuable coastline with poorly treated sewage while throwing away billions of gallons of a scarce resource.

Periodical Bibliography

The following articles have been selected to supplement the diverse views presented in this chapter.

Jim Carrier — "Water and the West: The Colorado River," *National Geographic*, June 1991.

Climate Alert — "Climate Warming's Effect on Mid-East Scarce Water Supply Could Undermine Security," January/February 1993. Available from 324 Fourth St. NE, Washington, DC 20002.

Benedykt Dziegielewski and Duane D. Baumann — "The Benefits of Managing Urban Water Demands," *Environment*, November 1992.

Michael Elliott — "The Global Politics of Water," *The American Enterprise*, September/October 1991.

Paul Gray — "A Fight over Liquid Gold," *Time*, July 22, 1991.

Robert Kourik — "Drip Irrigation: The Trickle-Down Theory of Watering," *Garbage*, May/June 1991.

Luna B. Leopold — "Ethos, Equity, and the Water Resource," *Environment*, March 1990.

William H. MacLeish — "Water, Water, Everywhere, How Many Drops to Drink?" *World Monitor*, December 1990.

Joseph P. Shapiro — "First Volleys of New Water Wars," *U.S. News & World Report*, May 30, 1988.

Leslie Spencer — "Water: The West's Most Misallocated Resource," *Forbes*, April 27, 1992.

Richard L. Stroup — "California's Man-Made Drought," *Liberty*, May 1991. Available from Liberty Publishing, PO Box 1167, Port Townsend, WA 98368.

Cass R. Sunstein — "Remaking Regulation," *The American Prospect*, Fall 1990. Available from PO Box 383080, Cambridge, MA 02238.

Curt Wohleber — "L.A. Thaw: Could Antarctica's Ice End California's Drought?" *Omni*, August 1991.

Dirk Yandel and Michael C. Paganelli — "California's Man-Made Drought," *The Freeman*, August 1991. Available from the Foundation for Economic Education, 30 S. Broadway, Irvington-on-Hudson, NY 10533.

How Can Water Pollution Be Reduced?

Chapter Preface

Many of the world's people do not have a reliable source of pure water. The river or lake they bathe in and drink from is the same water in which they dispose of their waste. Some rivers in Latin America, for example, are polluted by human waste one thousand times beyond the limit set for safe drinking water. But developing nations are not alone in suffering from polluted water. In many industrial regions, especially those in Eastern Europe, rivers are so polluted by industrial waste that even factories can no longer use the water.

Most Americans are fortunate that when they turn on their tap, clear, seemingly pure water pours out. Indeed, most of America's water is safe for drinking and clean enough for wildlife, agriculture, and recreation. Increasingly, however, America's water, too, is threatened by industrial pollutants and other forms of waste. As journalist Betsy Carpenter states in *U.S. News & World Report*, "Inept regulation, reckless land use and irresponsible handling of chemicals are all compromising the quality of the nation's drinking water." Excessive amounts of lead, pesticides, carcinogens, and microbes in America's water are believed by many to be responsible for numerous cases of gastrointestinal illness, lead poisoning, and cancer, and for damage to wildlife.

The Clean Water Act of 1972 and the Safe Drinking Water Act of 1974 were passed to prevent such water-related illnesses and to ensure that America's water is safe for fishing, wildlife, recreation, and drinking. The authors in the following chapter debate the effectiveness of such legislation and suggest ways to reduce water pollution.

*"The Clean Water Act has resulted in
tremendous improvements in our nation's water."*

The Clean Water Act
Reduces Pollution

ChemEcology

ChemEcology is the monthly publication of the Chemical
Manufacturers Association, a nonprofit organization of American
and Canadian companies that produce chemicals. In the following viewpoint, the authors state that the Clean Water Act passed
by the U.S. Congress in 1972 has reduced water pollution by establishing national water quality goals and authorizing federal
grants to encourage industries and municipalities to decrease
water pollution. The authors conclude that the act and its 1977,
1981, 1987, and future revisions will continue to help improve
the quality of America's rivers, lakes, groundwater, and wetlands.

As you read, consider the following questions:

1. What specific events led to the passage of the Clean Water
   Act in 1972, according to the authors?
2. The Clean Water Act established a federal water quality
   program. In the opinion of the authors, what were the
   advantages and disadvantages of this?
3. What challenges do the authors believe remain for reducing
   water pollution in America?

From "Water Continues to Improve Under Clean Water Act," *ChemEcology*, October 1991.
Courtesy of the Chemical Manufacturers Association.

Fish disappearing from rivers and streams. Lakes choked with algae. Beaches closed to swimming and fishing. Toxics and hazardous wastes casting a sheen on the waters in many cities and towns.

Twenty or so years ago, this was the sorry state of many of our nation's waterways. But during the early 1970s, a growing number of Americans began to recognize the damage that was being wrought on our fragile environment. The first Earth Day brought these concerns into the public spotlight, and the resulting outcry about the pollution of our country's resources, particularly water, soon captured the attention of public officials at all levels of government.

In 1972, Congress reacted by enacting the Federal Water Pollution Control Act, better known as the Clean Water Act. The goal of the new law was simple—water should support and protect fish and other wildlife and be clean enough for swimming, fishing and other recreational uses.

"The Clean Water Act was in response to a concern about some very visible pollution problems, including such things as rivers catching on fire and enormous fish kills of hundreds of thousands of fish that had become regular events on many of our waterways," explains Martha Prothro, deputy assistant administrator of the Office of Water at the Environmental Protection Agency.

The EPA and Federal Water Policy

While some individual states had clean water programs in place, they were not comprehensive or even consistent across the country. The Clean Water Act was the first federal program to focus on cleaning and protecting America's water. Responsibility was assigned to the newly created EPA.

The Clean Water Act established national water quality goals for planning and regulatory programs, and authorized federal grants to state and local water pollution control efforts. It also created a comprehensive system for developing water quality planning programs, water quality standards, permits for industrial and municipal dischargers, grants for construction of municipal wastewater facilities, and public participation opportunities.

The first step in enacting the Clean Water Act was to "tear down the state programs, to, in essence, (make them) mirror the federal program. This caused a fair amount of disgruntlement among state and local officials," explains Roberta Savage, president of America's Clean Water Foundation.

"But over time," she adds, "the benefits of having a national program have been demonstrated time and time again. And, of course, the infusion of federal dollars into the state and local clean water efforts has made a significant increase and impact in protecting our waterways."

The first 10 years of the Clean Water Act focused on the "obvious problems," according to Savage. These included effluent discharges from industrial plants and wastes from municipal sewage treatment plants.

Industry Has Acted

Savage notes that industry, for the most part, has done "an excellent job" in meeting the requirements of the Act. "Industry recognized that clean water was essential for a lot of the work that they do in the manufacture and transportation of products," she says, "and when (the Act) was put into place, industry set about meeting the requirements of the clean water programs.

"Industry has spent billions and billions of dollars since the original passage of the Clean Water Act to enhance and protect water and to meet the requirements of the federal statutes and the state and local requirements as well," Savage adds.

Cleanup Continues

For the past two decades, the main thrust of the Clean Water Act has been to prevent and clean up pollution from known sources, primarily industry and sewage treatment plants.

While those problems are far from solved, efforts dealing with point source pollution have generated significant improvements in our water supply.

ChemEcology, October 1991.

"The changes have been large in terms of costs," agrees Geoff Hurwitz, director of federal and state government relations for Rohm and Haas Co. "But I think the results of the investment have been extremely worthwhile in that, by applying technology from the end of the pipe, we have been able, in some cases, to restore our water bodies and secondly to protect our water bodies. So that cost certainly has been worth it for the environment.

"The Clean Water Act," Hurwitz continues, "especially the amendments that were passed in 1972, really represent an environmental statute that has worked. It is clear that in the past 20 years, discharges from point sources of pollution—point sources being largely industrial facilities—have really been racheted back to a high degree.

"I think every independent objective observer would say that the Clean Water Act has worked in reducing the amount of pollutants discharged from point source industrial facilities," he adds.

A 10-year assessment conducted by the Association of State and Interstate Water Pollution Control Administrators in 1982 supports this positive appraisal.

In the first decade after the passage of the clean water legislation, the nation's population grew by 11 percent and there was a tremendous increase in the use of surface waters for industrial and recreational purposes. Even so, according to the ASIWPCA study, 47,000 stream miles improved in quality, as did 390,000 acres of lakes. Approximately 85 percent of the major dischargers were in general compliance with their permit requirements, up 100 percent, by the 10-year evaluation. And 142 million people had received secondary or more advanced levels of sewage treatment, amounting to a 67 percent increase.

"We had made enormous progress over the first 10 years," Savage recalls, adding that she also expects that the second decade will show continued improvements. "We still have a lot of issues that face us, I won't kid you on that," she says. "But we have made great strides in cleaning up America's waterways and I think we should all be proud of the efforts we've made."

"I think that the Clean Water Act has resulted in tremendous improvements in our nation's water," agrees EPA's Prothro. "We have had considerable numbers of waterways restored to their beneficial use—they've been reopened to fishing and swimming and boating, and in fact, they have become so attractive that people are increasingly wanting to live near the water."

New Sources of Pollution

As industry and municipal sewage treatment plants continue their water pollution prevention efforts, those concerned with clean water have become increasingly focused on other sources of water pollution.

The original Clean Water Act has been revised and expanded through Congressional reauthorizations in 1977, 1981 and 1987. With each reauthorization, its fundamental tenets were strengthened and new requirements were added for such things as the control of diffuse pollution sources such as urban, rural and agricultural runoff, the protection of wetlands, toxic pollutants control and the protection of groundwater. . . .

"Our society is growing, our population is growing," explains Prothro, "and so we have diffuse sources of pollution, non-point source problems. They are agricultural activities, runoff from streets and roadways, runoff of pesticides from our lawns as well as our agricultural areas.

"Things of this nature are not traditional discharges from sewage treatment plants and industrial facilities that we have been accustomed, in the past, to being our primary problems," she says.

Non-point sources are generally credited with at least half of the nation's problems in terms of impairment of water use. Although most people associate non-point pollution problems with agricultural practices, nearly everyone, including private individuals, shares some of the blame.

"It is something that we are causing by our everyday activities," stresses Savage. "And that is more difficult to control because it means changing the attitude of the nation.

"We the people are the real bad guys in the environment today," Savage continues. "We take for granted that our water will be there when we turn on the tap; that when we flush the toilet the waste will go away and someone else will solve our problems for us. We have got to change that attitude, because there is a lot that we can do in this country to keep our water clean and safe."

No More Water

As they compile a national water quality assessment of the current status of surface and groundwater supplies, AISWPCA has identified key issues and challenges for the future. In addition to non-point source pollution, they include: assurance of adequate, safe supplies of water; development and implementation of programs to protect and enhance our groundwater; prevention of toxic pollutant loads to our aquatic environment; assurance of sufficient financial and professional resources to maintain and enhance current treatment facilities and management programs, and public awareness and encouragement of personal stewardship to protect our water resources.

Savage stresses the last point. "I don't think that people focus on the fact that we are drinking the same water that the dinosaurs drank in the beginning of our planet," she says. "The water is just recycled over and over again and it goes into our homes, it goes through our bodies, it goes through the earth and the atmosphere. There is no more water.

"So if we found the water beyond recognition or beyond use," she warns, "there's not going to be any more for us. We have all we will ever have. And if we trash our water supply, we as a people and we as a planet will not survive."

"According to the . . . Clean Water Act, . . . all releases of pollution into the nation's waters would end by 1985. . . . The goals still haven't been met."

The Clean Water Act Does Not Reduce Pollution

The Natural Resources Defense Council

The Clean Water Act of 1972 has been ineffective at reducing pollution because its goals were unclear and its programs voluntary, the authors of the following viewpoint maintain. Consequently, industries and other polluters had little incentive to stop polluting. The authors believe that the government's inaction concerning water pollution is inexcusable, and they demand that the Clean Water Act be revised and strengthened to ensure that the nation's water is clean and protected. The NRDC is an organization dedicated to preserving the world's natural resources and to educating the public concerning the importance of these resources.

As you read, consider the following questions:

1. What were the original goals of the Clean Water Act, in the authors' opinion?
2. What is the "zero discharge goal" and why was it not met, according to the authors?
3. Why do the authors believe it is important that the public know about the quality of the nation's water?

Excerpted from "NRDC's Campaign for Clean Water," *NRDC Newsline*, July 1991, © 1991, the Natural Resources Defense Council. Reprinted by permission.

It has been almost 20 years since Congress enacted the first comprehensive federal legislation designed to clean up the nation's polluted waters. According to the goals set in the 1972 Clean Water Act:

- All rivers, lakes, and coastal waters would be safe for fishing and swimming by 1983; and
- All releases of pollution into the nation's waters would end by 1985.

Unfortunately, the deadlines passed long ago—but the goals still haven't been met. In fact, the Environmental Protection Agency (EPA) has counted at least 17,000 bodies of water around the country that are still badly polluted. "Every year billions of pounds of pollutants—including toxic pollutants—are still reaching our nation's waters," says Bob Adler, an NRDC senior attorney with our Water and Coastal Program. "This pollution is taking a serious toll. It contaminates the fish and shellfish we eat, it taints our drinking water, and it endangers aquatic ecosystems.". . .

When It Rains, It Pollutes: Controlling Poison Runoff

The Clean Water Act includes enforceable requirements to control "point" sources of pollution, such as factories and sewage plants. But more than half of the water pollution today is caused by poison runoff that forms when rain or snow washes toxic and other pollutants into surface waters from farms, logging and mining operations, and even highways and parking lots. The resulting runoff can contain a polluted brew of heavy metals, bacteria, pesticides, and toxic chemicals.

So far, the only attempts to solve this serious problem have been through vague planning programs and voluntary controls—and they have not worked. "We have barely begun to fight against poison runoff, even though it's a major remaining source of water pollution that's wreaking havoc with the nation's waters," says Jessica Landman.

The solution: The Clean Water Act must be amended to contain strict, mandatory programs to control poison runoff.

300,000 Acres Lost a Year: Defending Wetlands

The nation's wetlands—aquatic ecosystems such as swamps, tidal marshes, bogs, and mangrove forests—serve many crucial functions. Among other things, they provide critical fish and wildlife habitat, including habitat for many endangered species. Wetlands also help to control flooding and erosion. And they help filter pollutants before these can reach other waters.

But our valuable wetlands are being destroyed at an alarming rate. More than half of the wetlands in the continental United

States have been lost since colonial times. And although the rate of wetlands loss has slowed somewhat in recent years, we're still losing wetlands at a rate of almost 300,000 acres each year—more than 30 acres per hour, according to the U.S. Fish and Wildlife Service.

Prevent, Protect, Enforce

Here are the changes that we are advocating in the Clean Water Act:

Prevent pollution and achieve zero discharge:
- Eliminate the use and release of toxic pollutants
- Prevent polluted runoff
- Eliminate toxic releases into sewage treatment plants
- Protect ground water
- Stop raw-sewage discharges

Protect critical ecosystems:
- Protect wetlands
- Protect aquatic ecosystems
- Prevent and clean up sediment contamination
- Keep clean waters clean
- Conserve and reuse water

Enforce the law/close the loopholes:
- Ensure public right to know
- Improve and enforce water-quality standards
- Strengthen enforcement and accountability
- Fund clean water programs adequately

These massive, irrevocable losses prove that the current law doesn't provide adequate protection of wetlands. But even the existing limited protections are being attacked by developers, the oil and gas industry, and big agribusiness. These interests have already introduced legislation in an effort to weaken protection for some wetlands, and to eliminate protection for others altogether. . . .

The solution: It's critical that Congress and the President get a strong message now that the law should provide *more*—not less—protection for wetlands.

Eliminating Toxic Pollutants

The "zero discharge" goal of the 1972 Clean Water Act to eliminate the discharge of toxic pollutants by 1985 was laudable, but unfortunately vague. Our society continues to use highly toxic chemicals, billions of pounds of which are released into water and other parts of the environment every year.

The zero discharge goal hasn't been met for a couple of key reasons. From the start, the EPA and state agencies moved too slowly in implementing and enforcing pollution controls. More important, they failed to develop a comprehensive program to prevent pollution at its *source*. Instead, they concentrated on treating wastewater before dumping it into rivers, lakes, and coastal waters, or on shifting pollution to other parts of the environment.

The solution: Congress must convert the zero discharge goal into enforceable requirements that industry eliminate pollution at the source, by reducing or eliminating the use of highly toxic chemicals and by requiring recycling and more efficient use of other materials.

Cleaning Up Sediment Contamination

Right now, EPA and state programs focus almost exclusively on pollutants in the water column. But many toxic pollutants, such as heavy metals and organic chemicals, don't remain dissolved or suspended in the water. Instead they accumulate in the underwater sediment, where they contaminate fish and aquatic life.

The solution: The Clean Water Act must be amended to require the EPA to issue strict sediment quality standards. And a program must be established to clean up contaminated aquatic sediments around the country.

Protecting Ground Water

Ground water is the source of drinking water for more than half of the people in the country. It's also a supply of water for wildlife, and a critical resource for crop irrigation, livestock watering, and other uses. For the most part, though, ground water isn't subject to the same comprehensive protection as surface water currently is. As a result, industries dispose of millions of tons of dangerous waste in ways that contaminate ground water. Other sources of ground water contamination, such as pesticide and fertilizer use, are almost completely unregulated, as well.

The solution: The Clean Water Act has to be amended to require the EPA and states to identify sources of ground water pollution and to protect ground water from all sources of contamination.

Enforcement and the Public's Right to Know

When the government doesn't take adequate steps to enforce the Clean Water Act, the public must have the right to take action itself, as NRDC has done all over the country by filing clean water citizens' suits. But these rights have been eroded by bad court decisions, and by inadequate citizen access to information about who is polluting which waters. Right now, the public doesn't even have the basic right to know, through mandatory posting requirements, which waters are too polluted for fishing or swimming!

The solution: Congress must increase public access to water-quality information, and strengthen the public's right to go to court to enforce the law.

Call to Action

The fight for these improvements in the Clean Water Act is going to be a tough one. But with enough support we can win strong clean-water legislation. "People *want* clean water," says NRDC's Adler. "We want to know that our water is safe to drink, to swim in and fish from. We want to be assured that our water ecosystems are safe for the wildlife that depend on them. This is the time to translate our concerns into action."

> *"Without adequate public investment, we may abandon some of the nation's goals for clean water and even see our recent achievements begin to erode."*

Increased Federal Funding Is Essential

Jonathan C. Kaledin

To help states and municipalities comply with the standards set by the Clean Water Act, the federal government provided generous grants for sewage treatment plants and other clean water projects. With the nation struggling under an enormous federal budget deficit, however, many of these grants have been cut or eliminated. In the following viewpoint, Jonathan C. Kaledin, an environmental lawyer in Boston, warns that this lack of funding threatens the nation's water quality. Without federal assistance, many cities and states will be unable to comply with the Clean Water Act and the nation's water supply will once again be polluted.

As you read, consider the following questions:

1. What kinds of problems are New York City, Los Angeles, Boston, and San Diego facing concerning their water supplies, according to Kaledin?
2. What is the difference between the Clean Water Act and the Safe Drinking Water Act, according to the author?
3. Why is the Environmental Protection Agency unwilling to force small cities to comply with the Clean Water Act, in the author's opinion?

From Jonathan C. Kaledin, "Priming the Pump: Paying for Clean Water in the 1990s." Reprinted by permission from *The American Prospect*, Fall 1991. Copyright 1991, New Prospect, Inc.

Turn on the faucet in most towns in the United States and you can drink the water with some confidence, if not always absolute security. In much of the world—India, China, Mexico—that simple routine of daily life is decidedly more dangerous. For recreation as well as drinking, Americans now enjoy water that is cleaner and safer than it was just twenty years ago. Thanks to state-of-the-art sewage treatment plants and other water pollution control facilities, we have made much progress in cleaning up our lakes, rivers, and coastal waters, reclaiming waterbodies that many Americans thought were permanently contaminated. Major problems remain, but the days are gone—for good, one hopes—when pollution on the chemical-laden Cuyahoga was so great that the river caught on fire.

Progress Is Threatened

These accomplishments did not come cheap or through voluntary action by the charitably minded. They involved large public investments and major expansions of federal regulation. Unfortunately, continued progress is now in jeopardy. For while federal regulation of water standards continues and has even been extended, federal financial assistance has slowed to a trickle. To upgrade their water infrastructure—sewage treatment plants, drinking water facilities, and other projects—scores of communities are facing huge expenditures. Until 1989 they could draw on a substantial program of federal grants; today all that remains of federal aid is a scanty loan program whose entire fund could be consumed by pending clean water projects in just one of our major cities.

Through 1998, for example, New York City alone has to finance an estimated $10.3 billion worth of clean water projects. Three other cities confronting multi-billion dollar costs—Los Angeles ($6-8 billion), Boston ($6-8 billion), and San Diego ($2-3 billion)—are under court orders to come into compliance with federal water standards. Since these and literally hundreds of other communities are building treatment plants or water supply facilities according to strict court schedules or administrative decrees, they simply do not have the option of putting off the work. And because state and local general tax revenues are unlikely to cover the costs, homeowners and businesses in many communities are in for a rude shock during the 1990s: astronomical increases in water and sewer rates. Around the country, water and sewer costs loom as the natural resources cost demon of the 1990s, a worthy successor to the energy crisis of the 1970s.

The surging costs of clean water are, unhappily, a representative problem of our times. Like the many roads and bridges around the country needing new investment, the nation's water

69

infrastructure requires large financial commitments, not just regulatory measures that express good intentions. As in other areas like Medicaid, the federal practice of maintaining and even extending regulation without providing commensurate financial support is producing fiscal nightmares for the states and localities and increasing pressure to abandon regulatory protections. The political effect is a kind of downward pressure throughout government to reduce public resources and social and environmental standards. If that downward pressure affects America's water, it will undo environmental achievements that affect all of us.

Expensive Water

The nation's accomplishments in clean water stem primarily from two federal initiatives: the Clean Water Act of 1972 and the Safe Drinking Water Act of 1974. The Clean Water Act regulates pollutant discharges to lakes, rivers, and coastal waters, setting as a national goal what is informally known as a "fishable and swimmable" standard. The Safe Drinking Water Act regulates public water suppliers to ensure they provide safe, high-quality drinking water. . . . With clean water infrastructure costs during the 1990s now figuring in the hundreds of billions of dollars, the issue of federal funding for federally required projects looms as a prominent issue.

No one doubts that the costs of clean water in the 1990s will be large, but experts disagree exactly how big they will be. Newly discovered problems seem to make most estimates obsolete by the time they are calculated. The one point on which everyone seems to agree is that if a particular figure comes from the U.S. Environmental Protection Agency (EPA), it is bound to be far too low. Nevertheless, we can compute a rough estimate by tallying three figures. First, the EPA puts the cost of work on sewage treatment plants over the next decade at $83.5 billion. Second, a group of municipalities, called the CSO partnership, that recently banded together to work on "combined sewage overflows" into rivers, lakes, and other waterbodies estimates that it may cost over $100 billion to implement current standards for overflows. And, third, an informal estimate from the American Water Works Association puts the cost of compliance with amendments to the Safe Drinking Water Act at approximately $120 billion.

These estimates add up to just over $300 billion, and that figure is probably conservative. The nation is just now beginning to focus on a host of new water problems that may generate additional costs. A good example is the discharge into waterbodies of excessive amounts of nutrients, such as phosphates, which cause algae to flourish and depress oxygen levels below those necessary to maintain a healthy ecosystem. Some states, anticipating likely new federal standards on nutrient discharges, are taking steps on their own. New York and Connecticut recently agreed to install nutrient removal controls in their sewage treatment plants discharging into Long Island Sound, in what might be characterized as a last-ditch effort to reverse the degradation of one of the nation's most troubled waterbodies. "We don't know where the money is going to come from," says Albert Appleton, New York City's commissioner of environmental protection. The work is estimated to cost $6 billion.

EPA Failures

The EPA has been roundly criticized by Congress, the General Accounting Office (GAO), its own inspector general and environmentalists for failing to enforce drinking-water regulations, especially in America's smaller cities and towns and in rural regions. In fiscal year 1990, for instance, 1 in 5 water suppliers violated a health standard or didn't adequately test water. Yet the EPA took enforcement steps against only a fraction of the most chronic offenders. The National Wildlife Federation's Erik Olson says the message is out to water systems that violating the law is practically risk free.

Enforcement breaks down at every level—local, state and federal. Many towns have simply refused to build expensive treatment plants, and neither the states nor the EPA have enforced compliance. As a result, water suppliers, large and small, violate standards with troubling frequency. For instance, the public utility in Hanford, Calif., population 33,000, still has not rid its water of naturally occurring arsenic, though it first violated standards more than 10 years ago.

Betsy Carpenter, *U.S. News & World Report*, July 29, 1991.

Although the clean water costs of our large urban areas have captured what little publicity has been generated on the issue, the nation's smaller cities and towns face problems that are, if anything, more staggering. An expensive clean water project spread over a small per-capita base spells real trouble. New Bedford, Massachusetts (population: 99,992), has about $500 million worth of clean water projects to undertake in the next five to six years. As New Bedford's mayor, John Bullard, put it, "You can't build a sewer treatment plant with 1,000 points of light. You need cash."

In the absence of significant federal or state funding assistance, the San Diegos of the country can turn (albeit reluctantly) to the bond market, raise the capital needed to undertake a clean water project, and pass the cost of bond issues on to water or sewer ratepayers. Because many small communities lack financial clout, they cannot gain access to the private markets that are the only source of capital finance when the higher levels of government leave the localities to sink or swim.

Small Communities Violate Standards

With a little prompting, the EPA's Office of Water Enforcement and Permits will admit that while it has energetically pursued compliance by large cities, the nation has between one to two thousand small communities still violating wastewater treatment standards. The EPA is reluctant to take enforcement action against these communities because the agency regards it as an exercise in futility. Compliance with the Clean Water Act would literally bankrupt many of them. Under the Safe Drinking Water Act, the picture is no better. The 1986 amendments call for rigorous new standards to take effect in the early 1990s, and public water suppliers who fail to meet them may have to build water filtration plants or covers for their water supplies. The costs are enormous—up to $7 billion alone for the EPA's recently announced plan to reduce the amount of lead in the nation's drinking water. Without federal help, there may be a "wave of conscious noncompliance" by small communities over the next few years, according to Jack Sullivan, deputy executive director of the American Water Works Association, which represents public water suppliers. Some suppliers might simply stop functioning, leaving people in those communities with no source of water except unregulated private wells. . . .

Perhaps the most ominous aspect of the current financial crunch is its potential impact on clean water standards, some of which have stood for decades. Calls for weakened standards have already emerged, driven by neither health nor environmental concerns, but by fiscal pressures. Without adequate public investment, we may abandon some of the nation's goals for clean water and even see our recent achievements begin to erode. Bottled water is now a fashionable taste. We must not allow it to become a necessity.

"There is certainly no environmental benefit to be gained to justify these large expenditures."

Increased Federal Funding Is Wasteful

William F. Jasper

The extent of the nation's water pollution problem has been exaggerated, William F. Jasper argues in the following viewpoint. Consequently, he believes expenditures by federal, state, and local governments have been wasted on water treatment projects aimed at complying with government regulations. Jasper maintains that government regulation of natural resources such as water is an authoritarian intrusion on individual rights. Jasper is a senior editor for the *New American*, a biweekly magazine of conservative political and social opinion.

As you read, consider the following questions:

1. Why have people willingly allowed the government to control the nation's water supply, in the author's opinion?
2. What problems have the citizens of Columbus, Ohio, and Anchorage, Alaska, had concerning their water supplies, according to Jasper?
3. What does the author believe will happen if Americans do not force their legislators to end needless spending on water projects?

From William F. Jasper, "Regulating Breath and Drink," *The New American*, June 1, 1992. Reprinted with permission.

It is difficult to think of any substances more ubiquitous than air and water, or more essential to human life. A government that controls the people's use of these basic elements wields power undreamed of by potentates of old. No free man would for a moment countenance subjection to Caesar for breath and drink, and no would-be Caesar in ages past would have had the audacity to propose such a transparent grab for absolute tyrannical power. But—might it be possible to so frighten a people with false stories of widespread, life-threatening contamination of air and water that they would beseech Caesar to regulate these life-essentials for the protection of all? Apparently so—and much more besides.

Bad News, Good News

As soil scientist Edward C. Krug has noted, "Starting with the first federal water pollution law in 1948, government has given itself increasing authority to regulate everything from noise to wildlife." With legislation passed in recent years, Krug observes that "government now has the authority to regulate literally every substance in existence." And it is exercising that authority with an increasingly heavy hand. In the name of the environment and public health, federal, state, and local bureaucrats are invading our communities, businesses, and homes, and bankrupting America with draconian edicts that cannot be justified on any rational grounds.

That's the bad news. The good news is that all of those alarmist scenarios of impending global ecologic doom and continuous horror stories of death-dealing carcinogens saturating everything we eat, drink, and breathe are daily being proven by hard science to be pure bunk. Contrary to the perfervid rantings of the green Luddites and their propagandists in the Establishment media, we are not destroying Mother Earth and poisoning ourselves to death with pollution.

Yes, pollution exists. Always has, always will. It is an inevitable result of human activity. (And not only of human activity, but of nature itself.) Nobody wants dirty air and foul water. The crucial question is what is the best path for human societies to take in pursuit of optimal environmental conditions, as well as other equally important objectives, such as economic and technologic development.

There will always be trade-offs, but, fortunately, these various objectives are not mutually exclusive. We need not impoverish ourselves by rejecting industrial-technological development for false "back to nature" solutions, nor repudiate individual freedom by embracing Big Brother statism to protect us from ourselves, as the eco-utopians propose. In fact, the myriad advances of modern science and technology, and the Western, Judeo-

Christian, capitalist, industrial system that produced these advances, have proven to be a tremendous boon to both man and nature. On the other hand, the socialist models advocated by the self-anointed "environmentalists" have proven to be colossal catastrophes for both humans and the environment.

© Mark Cullum/Copley News Service. Reprinted with permission.

According to Dr. Bruce N. Ames, "There is no persuasive evidence from either epidemiology or toxicology that water pollution or pesticide residues are a significant cause of cancer." Moreover, says the inventor of the Ames Test, one of the most widely used tests in carcinogen research, pollution of all kinds—air, water, food—"is probably almost irrelevant to causes of cancer and birth defects." This is so, he and many other scientists have repeatedly pointed out, because 99.99 percent of the toxins and carcinogens we ingest, drink, and inhale are natural ones we consume voluntarily through habits (such as smoking or chewing tobacco) and our choices of foods and beverages. But media overkill on dramatically exaggerated hypothetical cancer risks has given people the opposite impression. "The public has been inundated with stories in newspapers for the last 15 years about toxic waste dumps and all," says Ames, "and all of the supposed risk is based on really very flimsy evidence."

But scientific evidence, or lack thereof, has never stopped the

75

Green Lobby, its adherents in Congress, or the EPA [Environmental Protection Agency] regulators from foisting destructive mandates on the American people. Consider, for example, the plight of the people of Columbus, Ohio. In 1991 a committee headed by Columbus Assistant Health Commissioner Michael J. Pompili completed an exhaustive study of the city's costs of complying with state and federal environmental regulations. The total price tag is staggering: $1.3 billion to $1.6 billion over the next ten years. "Some perspective on the magnitude of these costs can be gained by realizing that entire city budget for 1991 is $591 million," said the Pompili report. According to the study, most of the mandated costs will go for compliance with the Safe Drinking Water Act ($110 million) and the Clean Water Act ($770 million). For this massive expenditure the people of Columbus will receive no known benefits. The inhabitants of hundreds of other towns and cities are in the same boat.

The people of Anchorage, Alaska, for instance, have reason to worry that the EPA may require them to build a secondary sewage treatment plant that would clobber them with $135 million in capital costs and an additional $5 million to $6 million annually in operating costs. Currently, under a waiver of Section 301(h) of the federal Clean Water Act, Anchorage is allowed to discharge its primary treatment sewage into Cook Inlet. Mark C. Premo, general manager of the Anchorage Water and Wastewater Utility, told the *New American*, "We have completed five years of testing and sampling of the Cook Inlet water and bottom sediments, at a cost of about $1 million, and have found no negative impact whatsoever. There is certainly no environmental benefit to be gained to justify these large expenditures [for a secondary plant]."

Lima, Ohio is another typical case. Accuracy In Media (AIM) reports that the city and its industries "have already spent $80 million for waste water treatment plants since passage of the 1972 Clean Water Act." New edicts "will cost the City of Lima $63 million in new capital outlays and its 60 affected industries . . . another $71 million, for a total of $134 million." According to AIM, "The average household [in Lima] now has annual sewage charges totaling $207; these will more than triple, to approximately $750. The annual bill for a large industrial user will increase from $102,000 to $383,000." Lima's mayor, David J. Berger, has denounced the EPA plan as unscientific, "deliberately ill-focused," and "a fundamentally hostile and exceedingly dangerous and costly program.". . .

The Deceptive EPA

The EPA, says K.H. Jones, "has purposely and cynically misled the nation. . . . The price of the EPA's misrepresentation will be paid by the American people, who will unnecessarily spend billions of dollars and possibly sacrifice tens of thousands of jobs to solve a problem that exists only in the minds of EPA bureaucrats and environmental advocacy groups.". . .

Unless state legislators and members of Congress start getting a very loud wake-up call now—as well as in the elections—from angry constituents, they will take the entire country down [a] socialist path.

"We are using too many chemicals . . . to remain content with the idea that our waterways and our air can dilute them. . . . We must produce and use fewer toxic chemicals."

Decreased Use of Toxins Would Reduce Water Pollution

Ruth Caplan

Ruth Caplan is the executive director of Environmental Action, an organization that promotes recycling and energy conservation and works to reduce solid waste and toxic pollution through research, education, and legal action. In the following viewpoint, taken from her book *Our Earth, Ourselves*, Caplan states that toxic chemicals have polluted America's lakes, rivers, and groundwater. While at one time it was believed that nature could handle a certain level of toxins, Caplan believes that this level has been surpassed, and that the environment and the health of humans and animals is threatened. Only when Americans reduce their use of toxic chemicals will the nation's water supply be clean, she concludes.

As you read, consider the following questions:

1. What facts does Caplan give to show that Americans are "addicted" to chemicals?
2. Why is the contamination of groundwater such a potentially serious problem, according to the author?
3. Why have laws addressing toxic pollution been ineffective, in the author's opinion?

From *Our Earth, Ourselves* by Ruth Caplan, copyright © 1990 by Environmental Action, Inc. Used by permission of Bantam Books, a division of Bantam Doubleday Dell Publishing Group, Inc.

Teach your children what we have taught our children, that the Earth is our mother. Whatever befalls the Earth befalls the sons of the Earth. Man did not weave the web of life. He is merely a strand in it. Whatever he does to the web, he does to himself."

When Chief Seattle of the Suquamish tribe, in what is now the state of Washington, said this to President Franklin Pierce in 1854, he had seen enough of the white man's ways to be concerned about the future of the environment. Seattle's eloquent plea for the new Americans to respect the air, water, land, and wildlife describes some early symptoms of our present disease; the plains littered with the rotting carcasses of a thousand buffalo shot from a passing train; the "lack of a quiet place" in our cities; destruction of forests; "the view of ripe hills blotted out by talking wires"; the disappearance, even then, of the eagle; the "stench" in the air.

The Horrors of Love Canal

We can only guess at Chief Seattle's reaction to a toxic waste dump such as Love Canal, which focused our attention on 50 years of careless production, excessive use, and indiscriminate disposal of hazardous chemicals. Beginning in the 1920s, an array of toxic substances was deposited in an abandoned canal between the upper and lower Niagara rivers near Buffalo, New York. With the postwar building boom in full swing, developers in 1953 filled in the rest of the old channel and constructed homes and schools on the site.

Over the next two decades, the buried chemical soup bubbled and oozed its way to the surface. Love Canal residents began noticing putrid odors and strange substances in their neighborhood and even seeping into some basements. In 1976, high concentrations of extremely toxic, cancer-causing PCBs were found in storm sewers bordering the old canal. It took New York's Department of Health two years to order the evacuation of pregnant women and young children from 239 homes in Love Canal. By then, Love Canal's "Tales of Toxic Terror" were mounting: babies born with abnormal hearts and kidneys and two sets of teeth; four mentally handicapped babies on the same block; rates of epilepsy, liver disease, nervous disorders, rectal bleeding, and miscarriage far above normal. Finally, the 900 families living in Love Canal were evacuated, and the long, expensive process of cleaning up the mess was begun. . . .

The Extent of the Toxics Problem

Love Canal [is one of the] most infamous toxic waste sites in our nation. But [it is] far from the only one: The overall dimension of our toxic timebomb is staggering. The Environmental

79

Protection Agency says there are as many as 29,000 waste sites that could qualify for its superfund cleanup program—which tackles only those toxic dumps that are considered the nation's worst. The Congressional Research Service of the Library of Congress estimates that our nation may be littered with as many as 300,000 hazardous waste dumps. Many are leaking poisons into the underground drinking water supplies that serve 120 million people, including 95 percent of rural Americans.

In its 1988 report *Environmental Progress and Challenges*, the EPA reported shocking statistics on the extent of toxic releases into the ground and water. Besides the 29,000 potential superfund sites, at least 180,000 pits, ponds, and lagoons contain chemical poisons; an estimated 500 hazardous waste disposal facilities and 16,000 municipal and private landfills contain toxics; and thousands of "injection wells" deep underground are filled with liquid wastes in an environmentally uncertain disposal process.

Waste dumps are merely one indication of the severity of our toxics problem. On a larger scale, we live in a society addicted to chemicals. In our nation, there are roughly 12,000 chemical manufacturing plants producing over 70,000 different chemicals, including 37,000 types of pesticides. Most of these compounds were on the market before federal controls were instituted and have never been adequately tested for safety. American industry each year generates more than 1 ton of chemical waste for every citizen—that's roughly 260 million tons a year. While chemical complexes and factories create a large amount of this dangerous refuse, the hazardous waste stream is fed by a wide variety of sources, including auto repair shops, the construction industry, dry cleaners, equipment repair shops, careless disposal of dangerous household products, laundromats, photo labs, and printers.

Our management of these various chemicals is marked by carelessness. Nationwide, there are around 5 million buried tanks storing petroleum products and chemicals. The EPA estimates that from 15 to 25 percent of these tanks may be leaking harmful substances into the ground. According to reports filed with the EPA, 19,000 industrial facilities released more than 7 billion tons of waste into the air, land, and water in 1987 alone. An additional 3 billion tons were sent to hazardous waste treatment facilities. . . .

Even "Clean" Microchips Pollute

There was a time when a community would fight to attract a computer factory—perceived as a "clean" industry packaged neatly in a low-slung, modern building. Since then, we've learned that not only does the manufacture of microchips help destroy the atmosphere by its heavy use of chlorofluorocarbons, but the process also produces huge amounts of toxic waste. Silicon Valley in Northern California, a center of microchip production, is experiencing rising rates of birth defects and cancer, as well as contaminated drinking water wells.

U.S. military installations and their stable payrolls are still very popular with local officials. But we've learned that, largely because of sloppy procedures with huge volumes of such chemicals as cleaning solvents, military installations are among our biggest toxic polluters. They have fouled the ground not only in this country, but around the globe. Part of Guam's water supply has been ruined by our military. Add this toxic waste problem to the chemicals mishandled by other U.S. agencies and we have the federal government as one of our biggest polluters. Nobody really has a handle on the dimensions of government pollution or how much money we the taxpayers will have to spend to clean up the mess. But shortly after Congress ordered the EPA to place federal facilities on its superfund cleanup list, the names of 115 of them were added to our "toxics hall of shame."

In our intricately connected "web of life," all these chemicals sooner or later turn up in the air, soil, groundwater, rivers, lakes, and oceans as well as in our food and ultimately our bodies. The polychlorinated biphenyl (PCB) levels in fish caught in the Great Lakes have gotten so high that people have been warned to limit their intake of these fish; pregnant women and children are advised against eating any at all. . . .

Tainted Groundwater

A 1988 EPA report states that "hundreds of different chemicals . . . could reach groundwater and potentially contaminate drinking water wells. . . . The agency's major concern is with man-made toxic chemicals such as synthetic organic chemicals that are pervasive in plastics, solvents, pesticides, paints, dyes, varnishes and ink." In fact, the agency examined groundwater in 38 states and detected the presence of 74 pesticides, 18 of them known carcinogens. Many of these, such as DDT, are pervasive. Even after DDT's use was banned, the pesticide was still showing up in one-third of the wells tested.

Because 90 percent of rural households get their drinking water from the ground, contamination of groundwater has the potential of causing many serious health problems. The EPA has tried to reduce the leaching of pesticides into groundwater, but as long as the farming industry is dependent on chemicals, the contamination of rural drinking water will increase. But even with reduced use of chemical pesticides, our groundwater will still be threatened by the many other toxics leaching into the soil from leaking underground storage tanks and illegal dumping of toxic wastes. . . .

Our profligate use and disposal of toxics threatens more than the health of humans. The EPA says that "potential impacts of groundwater contamination on the environment include adverse effects on surface waters and damage to fish, vegetation and wildlife. For example, 15 percent of our endangered species rely upon groundwater for maintaining their habitat."

"It's not my factory that's polluting the lake. . . . It's all those dead fish that're doing it."

Source: *The Workbook*, Summer 1990.

Our lives are filled with products whose manufacture, use, or disposal results in toxic threats. Behind our plastic jugs is a trail of organic chlorine compounds and organic solvents; behind common medicines we find organic solvents and residues and heavy metals like mercury and zinc; paint manufacture requires the use and disposal of heavy metals, pigments, and organic residues and solvents; leather production leaves behind heavy metals and organic solvents; and textile waste includes dyes, heavy metals, organic chlorine compounds and solvents. Other vast quantities of hazardous waste are created by the complexes that produce our metals, motor fuels, and pesticides. And, of course, the end products themselves must be disposed of when their useful lives are through.

We have responded to these threats with a patchwork of laws and regulations drafted and amended over the last 40 years. Some laws, such as the Clean Air Act, the Clean Water Act, the Federal Food, Drug, and Cosmetics Act, the Safe Drinking Water Act, and portions of the Federal Insecticide, Fungicide, and Rodenticide Act, have tried to protect the end points of pollution. By setting standards for our air, water, and food, it was hoped that the industrial behavior behind the damage would change.

All these laws approach the problem by defining allowable levels of pollution. The Clean Water Act, for example, allows industrial facilities and municipal sewage treatment plants to obtain permits to discharge polluted waste into streams, lakes, and oceans. It was based on the premise that if the concentrations of dangerous substances were kept relatively low, the waste problem would be taken care of by dilution in the receiving waterways. The Clean Air Act is structured in much the same manner. Unfortunately, this approach has not accounted adequately for the long-term cumulative effects of all these discharges.

Toxic Hot Spots

We've seen the development of "toxic hot spots" in our waterways—areas where the natural water was polluted to unsafe levels, even though each discharge pipe supposedly was meeting the requirements of its permit. It became clear that toxic substances our air and water were building up, not disappearing. Laws aimed at protecting food and drinking water ran into similar problems. The EPA has spent years trying to set standards for "allowable" contamination of produce and tap water. Because of the complexity of this task, very few contaminants have enforceable standards, and these standards change constantly as scientific evidence accumulates. Moreover, none of these standards takes into account the cumulative effect of all the contaminants we are ingesting. Because these laws have not stopped the flow of toxics into our environment, increasingly complex and expensive technologies are required simply to measure levels of dangerous chemicals in our air, water, and food, let alone repair the damage. . . .

Our nation's approach to toxics has been a dual one: "out of sight, out of mind" and "the solution to pollution is dilution.". . . The use and inadequate disposal of huge amounts of toxics being brought to public attention make it obvious that we are quickly exceeding—and perhaps already have exceeded—the environment's capacity to dilute these poisons. We are using too many chemicals and producing too much hazardous waste to remain content with the idea that our waterways and our air can dilute them, rendering them harmless. The obvious solution is that we must produce and use fewer toxic chemicals. We must practice the same source reduction that is so effective when addressing such environmental problems as air pollution and solid waste disposal.

There are many alternatives available that can reduce use of toxic chemicals. For instance, the 3M Company—Minnesota Mining & Manufacturing—has cut its generation of waste in half by using fewer toxics and recycling as many hazardous substances as possible. Not only is source reduction good for the environment, but it frequently makes good business sense. A company that doesn't produce waste doesn't have to pay for its handling, treatment, and disposal, and it doesn't have to worry about its future liability. 3M says that since beginning this program in the mid-1970s, it has saved more than $300 million. And it has saved its neighbors considerable exposure to chemicals.

Chief Seattle reflected a centuries-old culture that believed then, and still does today, that humans merely share the Earth. We must live in sustainable harmony with all else; we can only protect the land, not own it. Chief Seattle never saw a hazardous waste dump, a drinking-water well poisoned by chemical pesticides, or a huge petrochemical factory pumping toxics into the air. But his words, spoken long before we began fouling our environment with chemicals, gave us fair warning about our current problems: "Contaminate your bed, and you will one night suffocate in your own waste."

Individual Actions

The problem of nationwide toxic overload can seem overwhelming. Many solutions must occur at state and national levels that require changes in laws and policies. New chemicals must be more tightly controlled and registered. Waste management laws must be strictly enforced. Above all, chemical producers and users must be forced to find less toxic alternatives. . . .

Sooner or later most toxic emissions end up in water. Airborne toxics can travel hundreds or even thousands of miles, but eventually they are deposited in soil or water. For example, dangerous levels of PCBs in the Great Lakes have been attributed to air emissions from distant smokestacks. Toxics in the air or soil eventually work their way into groundwater or into rivers and lakes.

What can you do to find out whether your water is safe?

• First, find out the source of your water. Does it come from a private well or a centralized community supply? The answer to this question will determine whether there is any supervision over the quality of your water. Unlike community sources that serve more than 15 households, private wells are not covered by the federal Safe Drinking Water Act. For more information, contact the Environmental Action Foundation for a copy of its *Re: Sources* on drinking water.

• If your water is from a private well, it should be tested periodically for bacteria, metals, and volatile carbon-based chemicals such as chloroform, gasoline, and solvents. There are no simple tests for all pesticides. If you know a particular pesticide was or is being used nearby, you can ask the testing laboratory to look for its presence in the water.

• If you get your water from a community supply, ask the provider for copies of their monitoring reports, which are required under the Safe Drinking Water Act. Providers are required to monitor for only 22 contaminants, even though hundreds of others have been found in drinking water. Ask your provider to test for additional substances.

• Keep in mind that your water provider will be testing the water at their well or at the water-treatment plant, not at your tap. Have your water tested if it smells or tastes suspicious; if you live in an older building that might have lead pipes; if there has been any unidentified illness among several members of your household; or if you are concerned about a nearby contamination source such as a gasoline station, industrial facility, or landfill. For more information, obtain *Testing for Toxics: A Guide to Investigating Drinking Water Quality* from U.S. Public Interest Research Group, 215 Pennsylvania Ave., S.E., Washington, DC, 20003 or *Safety on Tap* from the League of Women Voters Education Fund, 1730 M St., N.W., Washington, DC, 20036.

Suspicious Bottled Water

• If you do turn up a problem in your water, switch to bottled water until you find and eliminate the source of contamination. But beware! Many bottled water companies are simply selling packaged tap water. Choose a brand that identifies the source of the water.

• A dangerous source of exposure to toxics is skin contact with contaminated water. If a test has confirmed the presence of chemicals in your water, avoid bathing in it or using it for washing dishes. Finding an alternate water supply can be difficult and expensive. In some cases, you may be able to recover expenses from the parties responsible for the contamination of your water.

• Get to know your watershed. This is the land area that overlies an aquifer or feeds a particular stream or river. Investigate land-use patterns for industrial activity.

• People have been able to organize locally to provide protection to their water that state and federal government have been unable or unwilling to provide. Under the Safe Drinking Water Act, an aquifer can get special protection if it supplies more than 50 percent of an area's drinking water. However, you must gather data to show this. Many localities designate "wellhead protection areas" and then prohibit such activities as underground tanks, landfills, and some industrial facilities from being located in those areas. . . .

All these changes would help clean up our toxic mess. But if there is one clear, pressing need, it is for all our environmental laws and regulations at every level to require the overall reduction of toxic chemical use at the source.

VIEWPOINT

"Artificial wetlands are turning household and even industrial waste into clean water."

Natural Methods of Treating Sewage Water Can Reduce Pollution

William K. Burke

Most of the sewage water in the United States is treated in conventional treatment plants that are often ineffective at completely removing pollutants from the water. In the following viewpoint, William K. Burke discusses alternative, "natural" ways to treat sewage water. Alternatives such as wastewater treatment greenhouses and artificial wetlands use microbes, fish, plants, and other aquatic animals to naturally clean water without chemical additives. Burke, a writer on environmental issues, lives in North Grafton, Massachusetts.

As you read, consider the following questions:

1. What specific problems are inherent in conventional mechanical-chemical water treatment plants, according to Burke?
2. What problem do toxic heavy metals pose for ecological treatment plants, according to the author?
3. Why does the author believe that some wastewater engineers are avoiding ecological water treatment proposals?

Excerpted from William K. Burke, "From Sewer to Swamp," *E Magazine*, July/August 1991. Reprinted with permission from *E: The Environmental Magazine*; subscriptions $20/yr., PO Box 6667, Syracuse, NY 13217, (800) 825-0061.

In 1983, Columbia, Missouri, opened a brand new conventional sewage treatment plant. Five hours after the city's 60,000 citizens flushed their toilets, the treated waste water flowed down Perche Creek on its way to the Missouri River. But that effluent, a mixture of water, human waste and common toxic chemicals killed most of the fish in the creek. The engineers who designed the new treatment plant tried again. The problem? Too much pollution in too little water. Their solution? More water. The city received $15 million in Federal grants to build a five-mile pipe from Columbia to the Missouri River. The mighty river would wash away the city's problems.

The planned pipe would empty out near the small riverbank town of Lupus, Missouri, about a mile above an island where the residents of Lupus spent lazy summer days picnicking, swimming and enjoying the sights and smells of the river. Doug Elley, mayor of Lupus, trained geologist and inventor of the "Sky Crapper" solar composting toilet, did not relish the prospect of swimming in 20 million gallons per day of partially treated sewage. He started searching for an alternative.

Someone gave Elley a copy of a magazine article detailing the work of John Todd, a Cape Cod, Massachusetts, ecologist developing waste water treating greenhouses. The greenhouses hold a series of aquariums where engineered ecosystems, selected groups of microbes, plants, fish and other aquatic animals, devour sewage. Early results suggested Todd's greenhouses could produce clean water—with no byproducts except lots of fish and snails.

From Susan Peterson, president of Todd's company, Ecological Engineering Associates, Elley learned that the experimental greenhouses are only one style of natural waste treatment. From Arcata, California, to Monterey, Virginia, high in the Appalachian mountains, artificial wetlands are turning household and even industrial waste into clean water. Arcata has a 154-acre wetlands park and wildlife sanctuary which serves as a living filter, purifying sewage and pouring clean water into nearby Humboldt Bay. Microbes clinging to the roots of wetlands plants digest the human waste that otherwise would have gone into a proposed regional sewage treatment plant.

A Cheap Way to Treat Sewage

Monterey's marsh was designed by Dr. Bill Wolverton, who developed his "marsh filter," gravel beds planted with cattails, bulrushes, and even canna and calla lilies, while working at NASA's Stennis Space Center in Mississippi. He created cheap systems for a number of cash-strapped southern towns that needed to clean up their sewage discharge, and for a four-factory chemical complex in Alabama.

Elley also learned that conventional sewage treatment is much more primitive than its elaborate steel and concrete constructions suggest. "The unfortunate fact of life is that, in every city, there is a pipeline going to a river carrying waste water that has been 'treated.' Now there's a word that soothes everybody's soul—but it's not what it sounds like. 'Primary treatment' is merely a process of *settling*—the lunkers sink to the bottom and the rest flows through. 'Secondary treatment' means bubbling air through it to give the microbes a few hours to decompose what's left. Then on to the river," Elley said.

Elley may be biased, but his description of modern waste water treatment does capture the essence of the process. He only left out the chemical additives, some of which kill disease-causing bacteria, while others remove excess nutrients, nitrogen and phosphorus compounds that cause algae blooms which smother fish and plant life, hastening the dirty water on its path to the nearest waterway.

Elley gathered about 150 like-minded citizens into Citizens Resolved Against the Pipeline (CRAP). Armed with Elley's research on the viability of alternative waste water treatment, and a passionate desire to find a greener way to resolve Columbia's sewage dilemma, CRAP marched into a Columbia City Council meeting. They spent three hours pleading that the council reconsider the pipeline project. But six of the seven council members voted to go ahead with the pipeline anyway. It seemed Elley had acted too late.

But Elley found a more powerful way to persuade the council—he threatened to take away their $15 million Federal grant. The 1972 U.S. Clean Water Act requires that, to receive Federal money, engineers must fully study and evaluate innovative and alternative technologies. Yet, the pipeline proposal contained no such consideration. "Not only did we have a problem and a solution, but we had the hard, cold fact that they could lose all their grant money if they didn't at least look at the wetlands alternative," Elley said.

A Popular Decision

Columbia agreed to consider wetlands treatment. Tracy Barnett, an investigative reporter for the *Columbia Daily Tribune*, wrote a year-long series of articles describing the pipeline controversy, and the successes of wetlands water treatment. When the sludge had settled, Mary Anne McCollum, the lone council member who had advocated taking another look at the pipeline, was Columbia's new mayor. Columbia killed the pipeline project and contracted instead for a 90-acre sewage-treating wetland designed by Dr. Robert Kadlec of the University of Michigan. That decision was popular; 95 percent of Columbia's voters chose to raise their sewer rates to fund the project.

The wetlands treatment project will supply water to 1,000 acres of Missouri River bottom lands being restored by the state's Department of Conservation. Bottom lands—swampy woods that hug rivers, lakes and creeks—are prime habitat for ducks, deer and many endangered plants. But they often fall victim to farmers and developers. Columbia's plan, a municipal improvement project that will actually improve bottom land habitat, is a conservationist's fantasy made real.

"The lay public seems to be slightly ahead of the regulators and possibly my colleagues in the engineering profession," says Woody Reed, author of *Natural Systems for Waste Management and Treatment*. "The public seems to find wetlands more appealing than concrete and steel. They sense the value, the environmental benefits."

Conventional Plants Are Ineffective

The brave new world of mechanical-chemical water treatment has sprung a million leaks. The $50 billion in Federal grant money distributed under the Clean Water Act has reduced pollution tremendously—it's been over 20 years since an American river caught fire. But that grant money has been used up, and few waterways can truly be called clean. "The number one source of water pollution in America today is municipal sewage treatment," says Kent Jeffreys, director of environmental studies for the Competitive Enterprise Institute, a conservative think tank.

Conventional waste water plants routinely release torrents of excess nutrients and toxic chemicals into harbors, bays and rivers. They also create 8.5 million tons of sludge each year, much of it laced with toxic metals. Advanced chemical treatment to reduce nutrients is expensive, while engineered wetlands can soak up nutrients for less money and create little or no sludge.

But Bob Bastian of EPA [Environmental Protection Agency] says that "much of the future of alternative waste treatment will depend on whether regulatory agencies push for compliance" with strict water quality standards. If communities trapped by low budgets and dirty water are allowed to build longer pipes to bigger waterways instead of cleaning up their effluent, ecological water treatment may remain a novelty.

Current mechanical water treatment plants also can't purify the toxic chemicals that flood into city sewers from homes and factories. Microbes that break down chemical wastes into simpler, safer compounds are present in conventional systems, but the waste water does not remain in the system long enough for the microbes to finish their work. Natural plant root systems provide the ideal habitat to give microbes more time to work.

"Plants do not remove the pollutants. Wetlands do not remove the pollutants. Microbes in the wetlands transform the pollutants. Microbes are the key," Dr. Donald Hammer of the Tennessee Valley Authority said in a speech to Seeds of Change, a Santa Fe, New Mexico, environmental consulting company working to spread ecological waste water treatment.

A Logical Process

Hammer has designed wetlands to treat the acid water that drains from mining operations, fertilizer run-off from potato fields, and even the waste water from a paper mill. He told his audience that wetlands waste treatment is not revolutionary, merely logical. "We have always dumped our waste into our waters. Microbes have always changed it. Our problems arose when we overloaded those natural wetlands and concurrently destroyed them by ditching and draining. And once we lost the buffering function of a natural wetland downstream from our cities, we polluted our water."

'Come on in, this is treated sewage'

© Liederman/Rothco. Reprinted with permission.

But while microbe colonies clinging to plant roots digest common carcinogens like toluene and benzene, toxic heavy metals like lead and cadmium pose a more difficult problem. Much ecological waste treatment research focuses on identifying plants that tend to accumulate specific metals. These metal-laden plants must then be gathered and stored in landfills. But that seems a cheaper and safer option than incinerating or burying tons of metal-laden sewage sludge, the current method.

Woody Reed did a survey of wetlands treatment systems to prepare his book's second edition. He expected to find 50 to 70 wetlands serving cities and towns. He found over 150. But ecological water treatment is not a routine option for engineers facing water quality problems. The need to adapt natural systems to local conditions makes them somewhat suspect in the highly standardized world of water quality engineering. "You can't open a textbook and find out exactly how to do it," Reed said.

Resistance from Engineers

Ecological waste treatment is an evolving technology, prone to successes and failures. Some wetlands systems have failed, others have not worked as well as their designers had hoped. "Wetlands are like big sponges soaking up and transforming pollution, but when 30 acres of wetlands get clogged you can't just wring them out," says microbiologist Alan Liss. And engineering firms, like doctors, must often face their failures in court. "It's easy for the general public to be enthusiastic, but if the system doesn't work, the engineer has the liability. That presses you to be conservative," Reed said.

Yet more outspoken advocates of natural water treatment feel more than engineering conservatism is keeping ecological water treatment from the limelight. Doug Elley pointed out that Black & Veatch, the firm that designed the Columbia pipeline project, is a multi-million dollar company with worldwide connections. Yet the firm's original assessment of possible solutions to Columbia's problem ignored the wetlands option.

"There is more money to be made in concrete and steel than cattails and ditches," Elley says. "In my opinion that's why the city wasn't made aware of wetlands treatment. That's why no towns hear of this wonderful solution to waste water problems. Rivers, streams and groundwater could be improved everywhere, but wetlands treatment isn't in the scheme of things because engineering firms are out to make the most money—and the more concrete, steel and gizmos they build, the more money they get."

Conventional waste water engineers are quick to respond that big cities don't have the time to let the hundreds of millions of gallons of dirty water they spew daily digest naturally, or land on which to build thousands of acres of wetlands. "I think [ecological treatment systems] are more suited to rural areas and the edges of urban areas," says Carmine Goneconte of Rhode Island's Narranganset Bay Commission. By this logic, ecological water treatment is fated to remain a cheap alternative for poor rural communities, especially in the South where there are no freezing temperatures to slow biological activity.

"I think that over the decades ahead we'll need to approach environmental restoration differently. We'll need to ask: 'What does this river need, what does this lake need?'" John Todd says. His words are a revolutionary gauntlet in the face of current waste water logic—which asks instead, "How much can this river, lake or ocean bear?" Todd hopes to make small-scale ecological water restoration efficient and attractive, and make big mechanical waste water treatment plants obsolete. . . .

Eventually the magic of John Todd's vision must be expressed in engineers' equations. Only then can his version of ecological engineering change how our society looks at waste water.

Periodical Bibliography

The following articles have been selected to supplement the diverse views presented in this chapter.

Jerry Adler   "Troubled Waters," *Newsweek*, April 16, 1990.

Betsy Carpenter   "Is Your Water Safe?" *U.S. News & World Report*, July 29, 1991.

Robert Griffin   "Introducing NPS Water Pollution," *EPA Journal*, November/December 1991. Available from Superintendent of Documents, PO Box 371954, Pittsburgh, PA 15250-7954.

Donald R.F. Harleman   "Cutting the Waste in Wastewater Cleanups," *Technology Review*, April 1990.

Charles W. Howe   "An Evaluation of U.S. Air and Water Policies," *Environment*, September 1991.

Debra S. Knopman and Richard A. Smith   "Twenty Years of the Clean Water Act," *Environment*, January/February 1993.

Wesley Marx   "Great Water Bodies at a Watershed," *EPA Journal*, September/October 1992.

Joan Murphy   "Uncovering Ground Water," *Public Citizen*, November/December 1989.

Daniel A. Okun   "A Water and Sanitation Strategy for the Developing World," *Environment*, October 1991.

David Pimentel and Marcia Pimentel   "Land, Energy, and Water—Keys to America's Future," *USA Today*, September 1991.

Robert Rackleff   "The Hidden Dangers of Oil Pipelines," *Vital Speeches of the Day*, February 1, 1992.

Curtis C. Travis   "Toxic Waste in Groundwater: Can It Be Removed?" *Journal of the National Institutes of Health Research*, February 1992. Available from 1444 Eye St. NW, Suite 1000, Washington, DC 20005.

How Serious a Problem Is Acid Rain?

Chapter Preface

Acid rain became a national concern in the United States in the late 1970s when Canadian officials complained that acid rain from American factories was harming Canadian lakes. Then in 1980, the U.S. Environmental Protection Agency declared that lakes in the northeastern United States were one hundred times more acidic than in 1940 because of acid rain. It appeared that both nations faced an environmental crisis. In response, the U.S. Congress in 1980 established the National Acid Precipitation Assessment Program (NAPAP) to determine the extent of the damage caused by acid rain. In the meantime, efforts by U.S. and Canadian leaders to reach an agreement on acid rain resulted in the Clean Air Act of 1990, which requires the United States to spend $7 billion a year to address the acid rain problem.

When the NAPAP study was completed in 1990, however, its results raised serious questions about the need for immediate action. NAPAP concluded that acid rain, although definitely a phenomenon, was not a major environmental problem requiring billions of dollars to remedy. "Acid rain does cause damage, but the amount of damage is less than we once thought, and it's much less than some of the characterizations we sometimes hear," stated James R. Mahoney, director of the study. The study found that fewer than twelve hundred U.S. lakes were seriously damaged by acid rain. While it had been feared that thousands of lakes would be fully acidified, these twelve hundred represented only about 4 percent of all of the lakes in areas where acidification was expected. Many environmentalists had predicted that the acidity in U.S. lakes would increase tenfold in a decade. But NAPAP determined the rate to be fivefold in two to five decades—a much slower rate affecting far fewer lakes. NAPAP found no evidence that acid rain had harmed forests or crops.

Reactions to the study were extreme. Some environmentalists, concerned about the effects of acid rain, castigated the research methods and the results and called for new studies. These critics complained that NAPAP researchers downplayed the study's Canadian results, which showed that 5 percent—possibly as many as fourteen thousand—of Canada's lakes were fully acidified. These results were treated separately and were not incorporated into the overall data. Some of the critics charged that NAPAP researchers, bowing to pressure from industry and pro-industry politicians, downplayed the severity of the acid rain problem. Other experts, however, applauded the study for finally discovering that the damage caused by acid rain was minor.

Clearly, the seriousness of acid rain is not easy to determine. Environmentalists, politicians, and others have varying opinions on whether a problem exists and, if so, how it can be remedied. Some of these opinions are presented in the following chapter.

"Acid deposition has damaged life in lakes and streams and corroded building materials and accelerated the aging of structures."

Acid Rain Is a Serious Problem

Cheryl Simon Silver with Ruth S. DeFries for the National Academy of Sciences

The National Academy of Sciences is a private, nonprofit society of scholars engaged in scientific and engineering research and dedicated to the use of science for the public's welfare. In the following viewpoint, excerpted from the book *One Earth, One Future: Our Changing Global Environment*, the academy's Cheryl Simon Silver and Ruth S. DeFries explain how acid rain forms and how it threatens lakes and forests and damages buildings. The authors maintain that acid rain could destroy hundreds of species of plants and animals if nothing is done to reduce it.

As you read, consider the following questions:

1. How does acid rain form, according to the authors?
2. What evidence do Silver and DeFries give to show that high levels of acidity harm fish?
3. What do the authors believe must be done to reduce acid rain?

Reprinted, with permission, from *One Earth, One Future: Our Changing Global Environment* by Cheryl Simon Silver with Ruth S. DeFries, for the National Academy of Sciences. Copyright 1990 by the National Academy of Sciences. Courtesy of the National Academy Press, Washington, D.C.

Even though the British scientist Angus Smith coined the term "acid rain" over a century ago, only in the last few decades have scientists recognized that widespread acidity in precipitation causes damage far from its source. Over large stretches of the world, acid deposition has damaged life in lakes and streams and corroded building materials and accelerated the aging of structures. In addition, it has become a key suspect in the declining health of some species of forest trees in North America and Europe.

Acid deposition results when pollutants, particularly oxides of nitrogen and sulfur, are emitted from smokestacks, smelters, and automobile exhausts into the atmosphere. These oxides are converted, through a series of chemical reactions with other substances in the atmosphere, to acids that fall back to the earth's surface dissolved in rain, snow, or fog, or as gases or dry particles.

Political Consequences of Acid Rain

The political tensions surrounding acid deposition arise largely because the effects of pollutants produced in one region can be felt in another. Lakes in far-upstate New York are acidified, in part, by emissions from the smokestacks of midwestern power plants. Acids that rain into Scandinavia originate in central Europe or the United Kingdom, and about 50 percent of the acid deposition falling in eastern Canada comes from the United States.

Acid deposition has been detected recently in other industrialized areas, including western North America, China, Japan, the Soviet Union, and South America. In some areas of Africa that are not heavily industrialized, high levels of nitric oxide and other gases implicated in acid deposition have been measured. Fires set by farmers to clear the forests and savannah are a possible source.

The main cause of acid deposition in the industrialized world is the sulfur oxide emitted to the atmosphere when coal is burned as fuel or when high-sulfide ores are used in smelters. The amount of sulfur in coal varies from deposit to deposit. The higher the sulfur content, the greater is the contribution to acid deposition once the coal is used as fuel. Not all coal is high in sulfur. Coal from the midwestern United States is high in sulfur—about 3 percent by weight. Coals from Appalachia contain from 1 to 3 percent sulfur. Western coal has relatively little sulfur, less than 1 percent. China, which is embarking on ambitious plans for industrial development, will build factories and power plants drawing on that country's large reserves of high sulfur coal. Coal that contains high concentrations of sulfur is also burned elsewhere in the world, such as in some Eastern European countries.

Nitrogen oxides are the second major source of acidifying compounds. Nitrogen oxides are emitted as a by-product when fossil fuels like gasoline, oil, and natural gas are burned. The amount emitted depends on a variety of factors, particularly the temperature of combustion. A large fraction of the nitrogen oxides responsible for acid deposition is emitted from automobiles and other vehicles. Stationary sources such as power plants also contribute significant amounts of nitrogen oxides to the atmosphere.

The Acid Rain Cycle

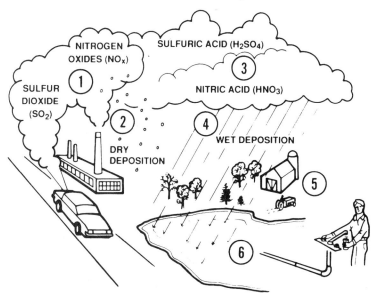

(1) Exhaust from automobiles, power plants, and factory smokestacks fills the air with sulfur dioxide and nitrogen oxide gases. (2) Some of the gases become attached to particles in the air and fall to the earth as dry deposition. (3) Great quantities of sulfur dioxide and nitrogen oxides mix with the moisture in clouds to form sulfuric acid and nitric acid. (4) These acids fall, with the rest of the water in the clouds, as acid rain, or wet deposition. (5) The acids poison trees, crops, and other plants. (6) Sulfuric and nitric acids build up in rivers and lakes, killing fish and polluting the eater.

Source: Acid Rain Foundation.

Scientists and the public in Europe became increasingly aware in the 1960s and 1970s that the amount of dissolved acids in precipitation depends on the direction, timing, and speed of air flowing over Europe and England. In North America and the rest of the world, concern took longer to set in. Throughout the early 1970s, research in North America on air pollution was motivated more by interest in the potential effects of atmospheric pollutants on human health than by concerns over the effects on ecosystems in water or on the land. Gradually it became clear that changes in the chemical composition of precipitation were having—or had the potential to have—significant effects on ecosystems. Since then, scientists have conducted millions of measurements and produced thousands of publications to understand the causes and consequences of acid deposition. . . .

Harm to Lakes

As researchers try to understand how acidification affects ecosystems, they are hindered by the lack of comprehensive biological surveys of large acid-sensitive areas, including North America. As David W. Schindler, an ecologist at the University of Alberta in Edmonton, Canada, explains, "As a result of never knowing what we had, we cannot know what we have lost.". . .

Much of the understanding about the effects of acid deposition on lake ecosystems has been obtained from studies in laboratories and artificial acidification of experimental lakes. . . . One of these lakes, "Lake 223," has provided especially valuable insights.

Lake 223 lies in a region with thin, sandy soils covered by pristine forests of jack pine and black spruce. It receives little acid deposition, and the surrounding watershed has very poor acid-neutralizing capacity. After 2 years of background study, researchers began in 1976 to acidify the lake experimentally, adding sulfuric acid incrementally until by 1983 they had lowered the pH of the lake to 5.0 from its original value of 6.8. In 1985, Schindler and his colleagues reported that the species living in the lake suffered the effects of acidification earlier than expected and that, even when the pH was relatively high, changes were extensive. The overall biological productivity and availability of nutrients were essentially unchanged, but a handful of species that were food for the healthy population of trout in the lake were eliminated at pH values as high as 5.8. When the study began, the lake supported a community of about 220 species. By the time the pH reached 5.0, fewer than 150 remained. (Even this number is misleading, Schindler says, because almost half of that number were acid-resistant organisms that had come in to replace ones that had been forced out by the acidity.) After 8 years, the trout—the top of the food chain in the lake—were no longer reproducing, and their mortality rates had gone up considerably.

Scientists believe that the number of species in a lake declines continuously with increasing acidity below pH values of 6.5 to 7.0 and that many species that are foraged by fish higher in the food chain are lost at pH values near 6.0. This disruption in the food chain means that large predatory fish can starve long before the direct toxic effects of acidification are evident.

"We are not losing hundreds of thousands of species, we are losing hundreds," Schindler says. "But in terms of the fraction of species that make ecosystems function, the relative magnitude of biological impoverishment in acidifying softwater lakes is probably just as large as in the tropics.". . .

Harm to Forests

Damage to trees from droughts, hurricanes, insects, and disease is as old as the forests themselves. The transport of pollutants from their industrial sources to stands of forests hundreds of kilometers away subjects these ecosystems to yet another form of stress. . . .

All trees experience stress in the form of diseases, insects, extremes in the weather, and competition with other trees for light, nutrients, and water. When the accumulated stress becomes too severe, trees become more vulnerable to opportunistic pests or injury from extremes in the weather. Eventually, the growth rate for the tree declines, and, if the stress is severe enough, the tree dies.

At high enough concentrations, air pollutants such as ground-level ozone and sulfur dioxide can damage a tree's foliage when they come in direct contact with it. Indirectly, acid deposition could deplete the soil of nutrients essential for the tree's growth, elevate the levels of toxic metals such as aluminum, and alter the normal functioning and growth processes. Because clouds can contain high concentrations of ozone and acids, and because soils at high elevations are relatively thin, the effects on forests are most pronounced at high elevations, where clouds and fog come in contact with the trees.

It is difficult to distinguish between damage to trees from natural causes and from air pollutants. Recent analyses, notably by the U.S. government's National Acid Precipitation Assessment Program, have considered forest damage in North America and attempted to unravel the causes. Red spruce that grows at high elevations of the northern Appalachians in the eastern United States has drawn special attention because analyses of tree rings reveal that in the past quarter century, the growth rate of the trees has declined substantially and over half of the mature red spruce trees in the high elevations of the Adirondack and Green mountains have died. In New York, Vermont, and New Hampshire, stands of red spruce began to decline between the late 1950s and mid-1960s. There is much stress from natural factors at high elevations, but scientists have now focused their studies on effects of acidic cloud water and ground-level ozone, which may compound the other stresses to the point where red spruce is unable to survive. On the basis of current scientific understanding, an interaction between injury from air pollutants and mites seems a likely cause of the spruce decline in the mountain forests of the Northeast. . . .

From an economic standpoint, corrosion of building materials is one of the most serious effects of acid deposition. According to the EPA, estimates of the annual costs of repairing or replacing structures damaged by acid deposition exceed $5 billion.

Marble and limestone, which is the second most commonly used building material in the United States, are particularly susceptible to acid deposition. The acids attack the calcium carbonate, the principal constituent of these materials. Limestone monuments like the Acropolis in Athens and the Jefferson Memorial in Washington, D.C., show signs of damage. Emissions from Mexico's refineries are corroding Mayan artifacts. In southwestern Colorado, air pollutants from several power plants and a nearby smelter are suspected in the quickening deterioration of ancient sandstone cities of the Ansazi Indians.

Of course, factors other than acid deposition contribute to aging and deterioration of materials, including sunlight, wind, and water. But evidence from buildings in areas receiving high levels of acid deposition indicates that the process is being accelerated. In addition to stone, acidic pollutants are also implicated in widespread damage to paint, wood, fabrics, masonry, concrete, and metals, though less is known about these weathering processes. The evidence is beginning to mount that rusted steel in bridges and corroded buildings are joining the list of the costs to society from acid deposition.

While researchers have been exploring the causes and consequences of acid deposition, engineers have been designing methods to control those emissions responsible for the acidity, and politicians have been debating the merits of implementing laws that would put these controls into practice.

Progress has been made over the last 15 years. In the northeastern United States, the sulfate content of rain and the concentration of sulfur compounds in the air have decreased, reflecting pollution control measures mandated by the 1970 Clean Air Act and efforts of individual states to limit emissions. Regulations for controlling emissions from automobiles have contributed substantially to the decline in nitrogen oxide emissions since their peak in 1978. But there is little doubt that emissions will have to be reduced much further to reduce the threats of acid deposition.

"Acid rain . . . is not an emergency."

The Seriousness of Acid Rain Is Exaggerated

Dixy Lee Ray with Lou Guzzo

While acid rain does exist, its severity has been exaggerated by environmentalists, Dixy Lee Ray and Lou Guzzo state in the following viewpoint. The authors contend that much acid rain research is flawed or inconclusive. Rainwater is naturally acidic, as are many lakes, Ray and Guzzo maintain, and most damage to lakes, forests, and buildings attributed to acid rain is actually caused by natural sources. Ray is a former governor of Washington and a long-time member of the zoology faculty at the University of Washington in Seattle. Guzzo is a radio and TV commentator and author in Seattle.

As you read, consider the following questions:

1. Why are people so willing to believe that acid rain is a serious problem, in the authors' opinion?
2. What natural sources of acid rain do Ray and Guzzo cite?
3. Why shouldn't the United States work to reduce atmospheric sulfur dioxide, in the authors' opinion?

An acid rain debate has been going on for more than a decade. Public concern in the United States probably dates from a widely publicized 1974 report that concluded "the Northeastern U.S. has an extensive and severe acid precipitation problem." Does it? Probably. Is rain actually acidic? Yes. Does acid rain, or, preferably, acid precipitation, really damage forests, lakes, streams, fish, buildings, and monuments? Yes, in some instances, but not as the primary or only cause.

Can the adverse environmental effects that have been attributed to acid rain, whatever the real cause, be mitigated by reducing the amount of sulfur dioxide [SO_2] emitted to the atmosphere from industrial sources? No. What evidence there is suggests that it will not make much difference. Is enough known and understood about acid precipitation to warrant spending billions in public funds on supposed corrective measures? Certainly not.

Errors in Research

Clearly, the U.S. Environmental Protection Agency has agreed with this assessment, for the agency's former administrator, Lee M. Thomas, said in 1986: "Current scientific data suggest that environmental damage would not worsen materially if acidic emissions continued at their present levels for 10 or 20 more years. Acid rain is a serious problem, but it is not an emergency."

That rain is acidic has been known for a long time. Among the first records are a reference to acid rain in Sweden in 1848 and a discussion of English rain in 1872. Sulfur dioxide was established as a possible cause of damage to trees and other plants in Germany in 1867. The commonly repeated alarm that rainfall has become increasingly acidic over the last 25 years rests for its validity on an influential and frequently cited series of articles by G.E. Likens and his co-workers published in the 1970s.

Careful evaluation by a group of scientists at Environmental Research and Technology, Inc., reveals that Likens's research suffered from problems in data collection and analysis, errors in calculations, questionable averaging of some data, selection of results to support the desired conclusions, and failure to consider all the available data. In a more recent critique, similar conclusions were reached. Besides analyzing Liken's methods of determining rain acidity, Vaclav Smil examines maps of the distribution of acid precipitation in the eastern United States between the mid-1950s and the mid-1960s, which had been prepared by Likens *et al* and publicized as providing "unassailable proofs" of rising acidity.

"In reality," Smil concludes, "the measurement errors, incompatibility of collection and analytical procedures, inappropriate extrapolations, weather effects, and local interferences make such maps very dubious."

A Need to Believe the Worst

How could such flawed investigations be accepted? As Smil aptly remarked, "The history of science is replete with episodes where cases of dubious veracity were publicized as irreproachable truths. . . . It may be irrational, but even in science, those who make the first and often sensational claim get much wider attention and are credited with more credibility than those who come later with calm facts."

It is an unfortunate human trait to prefer to believe the worst, especially in environmental matters. We really do like to be scared. We like to blame someone, to make sure that someone "pays." No one understands this better than those who call themselves "environmentalists." And so, when a public alarm is raised, whether the issue is pesticides, bioengineering, toxic waste, nuclear power, or whatever, plenty of spokesmen for so-called environmental organizations repeat the alarms over and over. Accusations of harm or wrongdoing, whether supported by reliable data or not, tend to carry great authority. The followup sober analysis and careful evaluation of data by scientists is frequently ignored or drowned out by the activist environmentalists, who shout "Coverup!" and "Whitewash!" So it is with acid rain.

To make an objective evaluation of the claims and counterclaims in this fractious topic of the acidity of rainwater, we should start with a brief, if somewhat superficial, look at water and rainwater itself. . . .

Rain forms when molecules of water vapor condense on ice crystals or salt crystals or minute particles of dust in clouds and then coalesce to form droplets that respond to the force of gravity. As rain falls through the atmosphere, it can "pick up" or "wash out" chemicals or other foreign materials or pollutants that may be present. Because water is such a good solvent, even in the cleanest air, rainwater dissolves some of the naturally present carbon dioxide, forming carbonic acid. Hence, rainwater is *always acidic*, or, if you like, acid rain is normal. There is no such thing as naturally neutral rainwater. . . .

Natural Sources

Sulfur and nitrogen compounds—the "acid" in acid rain—are produced naturally by the decay of organic matter in swamps, wetlands, intertidal areas, and shallow waters of the oceans. How much is contributed to the atmosphere from these sources is not known for certain, but it is considerable. Estimates of naturally produced sulfates and other sulfur compounds are from

35 to 85 percent of the total—a rather wide range. And naturally occurring nitrogen compounds are generally believed to be 40 to 60 percent of the total. Some experts go further and say nature contributes more than 90 percent of global nitrogen. Considering the additional sulfur that emanates from volcanoes, fumaroles, hot springs, ocean spray, and the nitrogen fixed by lightning, the generally accepted contribution from natural sources may be underestimated. . . .

Nature is responsible for putting large quantities of sulfates and nitrates into the atmosphere.

Man-Made Sources

But so, of course, is man. Industrial activity, transportation, and burning fossil fuel for commercial and domestic purposes all contribute sulfate, nitrates, and other pollutants to the atmosphere. Since passage of the Clean Air Act of 1970, there has been an overall reduction of more than 40 percent in factory and utility sulfur dioxide production. But as sulfur dioxide emissions decrease, nitrogen emissions are increasing, primarily from oil burning and the oil used in transportation.

Industrial society also produces other air pollutants, including volatile organic compounds, ammonia, and hydrocarbons. Any of these may contribute to the formation of acid rain, either singly or in combination. Further, some man-made pollutants can undergo photo-oxidation in sunlight, leading, for example, to the conversion of sulfur dioxide to highly toxic sulfur trioxide. But even this compound, should it be deposited over the ocean, loses its toxicity due to the extraordinarily high buffering capacity of sea water.

Another photo-oxidant, ozone, is possibly the most damaging of all air pollutants derived from human activity. Ozone accumulates in quantities toxic to vegetation in all industrial regions of the world. It is a product of photochemical oxidation between oxides of nitrogen and volatile organic substances. The latter may be unburned hydrocarbons—for example, from automobile exhausts in cars not equipped with catalytic converters—or it may be various organic solvents. Ozone is known to cause severe injury and even death to certain forest trees. The best known cases are the decline of white pine in much of eastern North America and ponderosa and Jeffrey pine in the San Bernardino Mountains of California. Ozone acts synergistically with other pollutants and has been shown to cause damage to agricultural crops when exposure occurs along with sulfur and nitrogen oxides.

Thus, singling out sulfur dioxide produced by human activities as the major cause of acid rain is not only a gross oversimplification, but probably wrong.

What about the dying forests? Here again the acid rain activists blame sulfur dioxide produced by industry. Like every other living thing, trees are not immortal. They, too, grow old and die. The decline of a forest may be part of the slow but natural process of plant succession, or it may be initiated by any of several stress-causing factors. Each forest and each tree species responds differently to environmental insults, whether natural or human. Professor Paul D. Mannion of the State University of New York, said this:

> If one recognizes the complex array of factors that can contribute to the decline of trees, it is difficult to accept the hypothesis that air pollutants are the basis of our tree decline problems today . . . [although] to question the popular opinion on the cause of our decline problems is not to suggest that pollutants do not produce any effect.

Widespread mortality of forest trees has occurred at times and places where pollution stress was probably not a factor. Declines of western white pine in the 1930s and yellow birch in the 1940s and 1950s, for example, were induced by drought, while secondary invasion by insects or other disease organisms is most often the ultimate cause of fatality.

Trends in Lake Acidity 1850-1988
(Mean pH values. Less than 5.5 = acidic)

	1850	1988	Change
37 Acidic Adirondacks Lakes	4.95	4.78	0.17
Nine Acidic Florida Lakes	5.11	4.81	0.30
All Measured Acidic Lakes to date under 5.0 pH	4.78	4.63	0.15

Percent of presently acidic lakes that were also acidic in 1850

Adirondacks (25 of 37)	67.6
Florida (six of nine)	66.7
Other New England (17 of 19)	89.5
Total	73.8

Source: Environmental Protection Agency, 1989.

Currently, the most widely publicized forest decline problem in the U.S. is the red spruce forest in the northern Appalachian Mountains. Few people now cite the widespread mortality in red spruce between 1871 and 1890. The dieback occurred at roughly the same time in West Virginia, New York, Vermont, New Hampshire, Maine, and New Brunswick, and then was attributed to the invasion of a spruce beetle that followed upon some other stress inflicted upon the trees. What that stress was is not clear.

Cold Winters and Forests' Decline

Today the dieback symptoms of the red spruce are most pronounced in areas 900 meters or more above sea level—an environment that is subject to natural stresses, such as wind, winter cold, and nutrient-poor soils, as well as possible high levels of pollutants, heavy metals, and acidity in the clouds that often envelop the forest. The relative importance of each of these stresses has not been rigorously investigated.

The affected trees grow in one of the windiest locations in North America. It is known that wind can dry out or even remove red spruce foliage, especially if rime ice has formed. It can also cause root damage by excessive tree movements. Tree ring analyses indicate a possible relation between recent cold winters and decline. The abnormal cold extending into spring may have caused the trees to be more susceptible to the adverse effects of pollutants.

Arthur H. Johnson and Samuel B. MacLaughlin, who have studied tree rings and the red spruce forest decline, wrote this in their *Acid Deposition: Long Term Trends*: "There is no indication now that acidic deposition is an important factor in red spruce decline. . . . The abrupt and synchronous changes in ring width and wood density patterns across such a wide area seem more likely to be related to climate than to air pollution.". . .

Effects on Lakes and Fish

There are three kinds of naturally occurring acidic lakes. First are those associated with inorganic acids in geothermal areas, like Yellowstone Park, and sulfur springs, with a pH of 2.0 to 3.0. Then there are those found in peat lands, cypress swamps, and rain forests, where the acidity is derived from organic acids leached from humus and decaying vegetation, with pH 3.5 to 5. Finally, there are those in areas of weather-resistant granitic or silicious bedrock, which are the only ones involved in the acid rain question.

In these lakes and streams, the absence of carbonate rocks means little natural buffering capacity. This type of naturally acidic lake is common in large areas of eastern Canada and the northeastern United States, where glaciers exposed granitic bedrock during the last period of glaciation. The lakes are called "sensitive" because they may readily become further acidified with adverse effects on aquatic organisms, of which fish are the most important to man. Indeed, the most widely proclaimed complaint about acid deposition is the reduction or elimination of fish populations.

But again, this is not a recent phenomenon. Dead lakes are not new. A study by the New York State Department of Environmental Conservation reveals that the stocking of fish in 12 lakes was attempted and failed as early as the 1920s. Of course, many people did catch fish in the 1920s and 1930s in lakes where fish are not available today. But the fact is that during those years many of the Adirondack lakes were being stocked annually by the Fish and Game Commission. Fish did not propagate, and the stocking program was discontinued about 1940.

In the United States, 219 lakes have been identified as too acidic to support fish. Two hundred and six of these lakes are in the Adirondacks, but they account for only four percent of the lake surface of New York State. This, then, is hardly a national problem; it is local. The same applies to southeastern Canada, which has the highest percentage of acid lakes. . . .

Effects on Man-Made Structures

The impact of airborne pollutants and acid rain on deterioration of buildings, monuments, and man-made materials is also predominantly a local phenomenon. It is at least as complex as the effects on the natural environment. And, like forests and lakes, every site is specific and every material different. Few generalizations are possible. Fewer still stand up under careful scrutiny. Of course metals corrode, marble and limestone weather, masonry and concrete deteriorate, paint erodes, and so on. But the conditions and substances that lead to loss of integrity vary widely. Perhaps the only statements that can be made are that moisture is essential, that deterioration results more from acid deposition than from acid rain, and that local pollutants are more important than pollutants possibly transported from far away.

Yet the belief persists that acid rain from "someplace else" is destroying cultural monuments and buildings. Perhaps the most egregious example is the damage to the granite Egyptian obelisk, "Cleopatra's Needle," which has been in New York's Central Park since 1881. It's been said that "the city's atmosphere has done more damage than three and a half millenia in the desert, and in another dozen years the hieroglyphs will disappear." A careful study of the monument's complex history, however, makes it clear that the damage can be attributed to advanced salt decay from the "salting" of icy streets during winter, the high humidity of the New York climate in the summer, and unfortunate attempts at preservation. There is no question but that acid deposition causes incremental damage to materials, but far more research is needed before reliable surface protection systems can be developed.

Congress should be very cautious about committing public funds to "solutions" to an ill-defined problem. At best, proposed federal programs constitute, in the words of Dr. S. Fred Singer of the National Advisory Committee on Oceans and Atmosphere, "a multibillion dollar solution to a multimillion dollar problem.". . .

Eliminating SO₂ Is Not the Answer

Does our knowledge about acid rain, its origin, extent, and effect on the environment, warrant spending 2.5 billion or more taxpayer dollars on a program to reduce atmospheric SO_2? There are plenty of good reasons to cut down on the amount of sulfur and other pollutants that pour into the atmosphere, but to use acid rain as an excuse and to intimate that if SO_2 is eliminated then acid rain will disappear is not only simplistic and unscientific, it is grossly misleading, as well. . . .

Atmospheric SO_2—which is widely assumed, but certainly not proved, to be the primary cause of acid rain—has been reduced by more than 15 percent since 1973. Yet the acidity of rainwater remains the same. Similar results with even greater SO_2 reductions (30 percent since 1970) are reported from Great Britain and Scandinavia. Most knowledgeable scientists agree that about half of all atmospheric sulfur worldwide comes from natural causes, including volcanic eruptions. We also know that rainwater is naturally acidic; that its acidity can be increased by pollutants; that the amount of acid deposition—which is much more important than the pH of rainwater—and the natural pH of soils differs widely across the United States; and that naturally occurring limestone, the liming of agricultural soil, and the use of ammonia-based fertilizers buffer acid deposition. . . .

What to do? Any federal funds that will be spent on acid rain should be spent on research—not on boondoggles to satisfy the mindless cries to "do something" from those who would substitute passion for science.

"The acid rain legislation was indeed a response commensurate to the environmental threats at hand."

Government Measures to Reduce Acid Rain Are Necessary

Ned Helme and Chris Neme

In 1990, the Congress and President George Bush passed the acid rain program as an amendment to the Clean Air Act. The program aims to reduce national sulfur dioxide emissions by ten million tons, thereby reducing acid rain. In the following viewpoint, Ned Helme and Chris Neme applaud the government's efforts at reducing acid rain. Such efforts are necessary, the authors believe, to protect lakes and forests. Helme is the executive director and Neme is a senior policy analyst of the Alliance for Acid Rain Control, an organization that works to reduce acid rain and to inform the public about the threat it poses.

As you read, consider the following questions:

1. What role does coal play in America's acid rain problem, according to the authors?
2. Why do some critics of the acid rain legislation believe it was unnecessary, according to Helme and Neme?
3. What do the authors believe will be the economic benefits of acid rain legislation?

Reprinted from Ned Helme and Chris Neme, "Acid Rain: The Problem," *EPA Journal*, January/February 1991.

Acid deposition, popularly known as acid rain, has long been suspected of damaging lakes, streams, forests, and soils, decreasing visibility, corroding monuments and tombstones, and potentially threatening human health in North America and Europe. The National Academy of Sciences and other leading scientific bodies first gave credence to these concerns in the early 1980s when they suggested that emissions of sulfur dioxide from electric power plants were being carried hundreds of miles by prevailing winds, being transformed in the atmosphere into sulfuric acid, falling into pristine lakes, and killing off aquatic life.

The Culprit: Sulfur Dioxide

Acid rain in the United States is caused mainly by man-made pollutants. It results primarily from the reaction of sulfur dioxide and nitrogen oxides with other substances in the atmosphere. Coal-burning electric power plants are the primary source of sulfur dioxide and a leading source of nitrogen oxides.

Sulfur dioxide, the most important of these two pollutants, is created when the sulfur in coal is released during combustion and reacts with oxygen in the air. The amount of sulfur dioxide created depends on the amount of sulfur in the coal. All coal contains some sulfur, but the amount varies significantly depending on where the coal is mined.

The sulfur content of western coal, for example, is typically very low—about 0.5 percent. Western states produce about 40 percent of the coal currently sold to electric utilities. The East produces both low-sulfur and high-sulfur coal. Low-sulfur coal from southern Appalachia (typically about 1 percent sulfur) currently commands about 20 percent of the national utility market. High-sulfur coal from northern Appalachia and the lower midwestern states (about 2 to 3 percent sulfur) accounts for most of the rest of the sales to electric utilities.

Today, the United States gets more than 55 percent of its electricity from coal and the trend is upward. Utility coal consumption has nearly doubled since the mid-1970s to more than 750 million tons a year, about 85 percent of total U.S. coal consumption. Although acid rain emissions have actually decreased somewhat over the last 15 years, because of the installation of some pollution controls and greater reliance on low-sulfur coal, emissions were predicted to increase again for the next decade or two in the absence of acid-rain control requirements.

Acid rain doesn't stop at political boundaries. High-sulfur coal-burning power plants in the Ohio River Valley and lower Midwest contribute to acidification of lakes as far away as upstate New York, New England, and Canada. Roughly half of the acid rain in Canada results from pollution in the United States.

In our own Adirondack Mountains—a particularly vulnerable area—up to 15 percent of medium and large lakes (greater than 10 acres) are chronically acidic due primarily to acid rain; more than 25 percent of small lakes (2 to 10 acres) in the Adirondacks are likewise chronically acidic due largely to acid rain. A smaller percentage of lakes and streams in New England, the upper Midwest, and the Appalachian Mountains are chronically acidic.

Many other lakes and streams experience episodic acidity. When acidic snow melts in the spring, significant adverse effects on aquatic life can result. Perhaps of even greater long-term concern is the number of lakes and streams that have little acid-buffering capacity and are susceptible to future acidification in the United States. Roughly 20 percent of lakes and streams fit this description, according to a draft report by the National Acid Precipitation Assessment Program (NAPAP), a 10-year scientific study sponsored by Congress.

Acid rain also adversely affects the environment beyond the acidification of lakes and streams—a critical point often lost in the controversy over acid rain policy. For example, acid rain has damaged high-elevation spruce forests in the eastern United States, and it has also accelerated the corrosion of buildings and monuments.

Acid rain has contributed to reduced visibility at scenic vistas throughout North America. Byproducts of sulfur dioxide, acid rain's principal precursor, are recognized as major contributors to regional haze in the East and parts of the West. These byproducts, known as sulfates, have received a great deal of attention lately because of the impaired visibility at a number of U.S. national parks. At times, the sulfate pollution is so great that people can't see the bottom of the Grand Canyon or across Virginia's Shenandoah Valley.

More recently, it has become apparent that acid rain facilitates the accumulation of mercury, a toxic metal, in fish. Studies show correlation between the acidity of lake water and high mercury levels in fish, although the biological and chemical processes underlying this relationship are not fully understood. Elevated levels of mercury have led many states—particularly the upper Great Lakes states of Minnesota, Wisconsin, and Michigan—to advise against eating sport fish caught in their inland lakes. In Michigan, the public health advisory extends to every one of roughly 10,000 inland lakes in the state.

Also, there is growing concern about the potential health risks associated with acid rain. Recent reports suggest, for example, that downwind derivatives of sulfur dioxide, known as acid aerosols, may pose serious health threats throughout the eastern United States. Inhalation of acid aerosols may lead to bronchitis in children and decreased lung function in adults, particularly asthmatics. Controlling acid rain will play an important role in reducing these risks.

Creating Solutions Proved Difficult

Despite growing awareness of the acid rain problem among citizens and public officials, designing an effective strategy to control it proved to be one of the nation's most intractable environmental policy problems. The Congressional debate bogged down for years in a sometimes acrimonious political stalemate.

The mid-1980s saw renewed efforts to resolve the debate. In 1985, for example, a bi-partisan group of state governors concluded that the environmental threats posed by acid rain were well-enough established to warrant remedial action. The group formed the Alliance for Acid Rain Control to seek a pragmatic, consensus-based solution that could win broad support from government, industry, and the environmental community.

In 1990, Congress finally enacted long-overdue clean air legislation. The acid rain program, part of the Clean Air Act Amendments of 1990, embodies the major policy principles supported by the Alliance for Acid Rain Control: reducing national sulfur-dioxide emissions by 10 million tons below 1980 levels, giving industry the flexibility to choose the cheapest means for reducing emissions and making polluters pay for their own cleanup.

Nevertheless, some producers of high-sulfur coal and some midwestern utilities still contend that the American public was misled when acid rain legislation was enacted. Most recently they have argued that the final NAPAP report concludes that acid rain is not a catastrophic environmental problem. The NAPAP study concluded that the number of acidic lakes has grown only slightly over the last 10 years and that forest damage from acid rain has been limited to high-elevation stands.

These arguments received a wide public airing on CBS's "60 Minutes." Unfortunately, the program's coverage seemed to imply that legislation and remedial action were needed *only* if acid rain is an environmental "catastrophe." This approach misses the main point: If acidification of lakes has not become much worse over the last decade, this does not negate the need to address the problem we already had 10 years ago.

Benefits Outweigh Costs

Acid rain control will provide significant environmental benefits. In 1989 testimony before Congress, NAPAP Director Jim Mahoney agreed that a 10-million-ton emission reduction "would benefit aquatic resources and would mitigate other environmental effects caused by acidic deposition and its precursors."

"The only question," as he later noted for the *Washington Post*, "is how much reduction is appropriate and how much benefit are we going to get from the cost."

All available evidence suggests that the acid rain legislation was indeed a response commensurate to the environmental threats at hand. An analysis by Resources for the Future, a leading research organization, suggests that the benefits of acid rain control will be worth roughly $5 billion a year, about 50 percent greater than the costs of controlling acid rain. Similarly, a 1988 EPA [Environmental Protection Agency] analysis found that the benefits of reducing sulfur dioxide emissions outweigh the costs.

A decade of research has refined our scientific understanding of acid rain. But nothing we have learned in the past decade contradicts the basic conclusion that the combined impacts of acid rain are significant enough to warrant measured action to reduce it. President George Bush and the Congress should be congratulated for taking such action.

> *"On all accounts the 1990 Clean Air Act (CAA) treatment of acid rain . . . involves 'throwing good money after bad.'"*

Government Measures to Reduce Acid Rain Are Unnecessary

J. Laurence Kulp

J. Laurence Kulp, an affiliate professor at the University of Washington and a consultant in environmental and energy affairs, was the director of research for the National Acid Precipitation Assessment Program from 1985 to 1987. NAPAP was created in 1980 to determine the seriousness of America's acid rain problem. In the following viewpoint, Kulp asserts that NAPAP found acid rain to be a minor problem. Consequently, he believes the 1990 acid rain amendment to the Clean Air Act, which would spend $100 billion to reduce acid rain, is unnecessary and a waste of money.

As you read, consider the following questions:

1. On what two false assumptions is the 1990 acid rain legislation based, according to Kulp?
2. In addition to the cost, what other detriments does the author see to the 1990 legislation?
3. What solution to the acid rain problem does Kulp advocate?

Excerpted from J. Laurence Kulp, "Acid Rain: An Environmental Problem?" This article appeared in the November 1991 issue, and is reprinted with permission of, *The World and I*, a publication of The Washington Times Corporation, copyright © 1992.

To intelligently allocate our limited resources for the improvement of our environment, we need to understand the causes and effects of any potential threat. We also need to ensure that the benefits derived from the control of that threat significantly outweigh the costs. While research enables us to analyze the damage caused by a given level of pollution, technological development enables us to lower the pollution or lower the cost for the current level of control. Economic study can help us quantify the costs of control or mitigation and the resulting environmental benefits.

There are numerous examples where misguided legislation, regulation, administrative policy, or environmentalist propaganda has resulted in significant financial losses for the national economy. Some examples are: the Alar scare that threatened apple growers; the "endangered" snail darter that delayed completion of a major dam on the Tennessee River; the Seabrook nuclear reactor delayed by antinuclear activists; harmless dioxin in paper products; the trivial improvement in visibility for a few days in winter by spending $2-3 billion in controls on a coal plant near the Grand Canyon; and the PCB scare. In each case science was either ignored or distorted, or the costs of control were enormous compared to the small benefits. And in every instance hundreds of millions to billions of dollars were essentially wasted.

Yet all these examples pale into insignificance when compared with the $100 billion required by the 1990 Clean Air Act to solve the acid rain problem. . . .

The 1990 Amendment to the Clean Air Act

In the fall of 1990 Congress amended the Clean Air Act to require a reduction in emissions that produce acid rain by 10 million tons per year by about the year 2000, or about half the current emissions. The target is to reduce average emissions from all large utility plants to 1.2 pounds of sulfur dioxide per million Btu (British thermal units) of heat energy. The cost of retrofitting older generating plants with scrubbers to meet this requirement is estimated to be about $100 billion over the next 20 years.

This extremely costly "crash" program was based on two false assumptions: (1) acid rain at its current level has produced an ecological "crisis"; and (2) the situation is rapidly deteriorating so that action was urgent. Virtually no attention was paid to the results of the ten-year, half-billion-dollar NAPAP study that Congress had commissioned in 1980. Compared with the $100 billion cost, it is hard to identify $1 billion in benefits, even using the most supportive assumptions.

Beyond the negligible cost-benefit ratio of this program, the strategy mandated by the Clean Air Act amendments has several other negative aspects. Retrofitting older plants will cause further investment to extend their useful lives, thereby burdening the utilities with inefficient plants long into the future—this instead of investing in new technology with much higher thermal efficiencies.

Ignoring Scientific Facts

On October 26th, 1992, Environmental Protection Agency officials issued a series of regulations designed to combat the acid rain problem they claim is devastating lakes, streams, and forests in the northeastern United States and southeastern Canada. Their main target is sulfur dioxide emissions from over 100 coal-burning power plants in the East and Midwest. Reductions must total 3.5 million tons by 1995, and an additional 6.5 million tons (a combined total from nearly 1,000 plants nationally) after the year 2000. The rules mark the beginning of a flood of new regulations mandated by the 1990 Clean Air Act. . . .

The greatest problem with all of this costly bureaucratic rule-making is that it stems from total falsehoods. Real scientists—not the bureaucrats and politicians from the EPA—know from more than ten years of intensive study that no lakes and streams have become fish-less because of acid produced from power plant and auto emissions. They know that many acidic lakes in the Adirondack area of New York have been highly acidic for centuries. In fact, fossil organisms and chemicals extracted from some Adirondack lake sediments demonstrate that many of these lakes have almost always been highly acidic and without fish. After ten years of study, the National Acid Precipitation Assessment Program concluded in 1990 that no man-made activity has been responsible for the acidity that exists in some waterways.

John F. McManus, *The New American*, December 14, 1992.

Another drawback is the electrical energy needed to power the scrubbers, so that each plant will generate less electrical power per ton of coal than it did before, at a time when electrical demand is steadily increasing. The scrubbers, moreover, produce a huge amount of sulfate sludge, which causes a long-term solid waste disposal problem. Finally, investing in new technology in new plants would ultimately produce much lower emissions, thus yielding superior environmental conditions. It would reduce the acidity of rain to near natural background levels.

As such, on all accounts the 1990 Clean Air Act (CAA) treatment of acid rain is undesirable. It basically involves "throwing good money after bad."

A far more economic policy would be to allow the old plants to operate to the end of their economic life; but require new plants to meet even more stringent emission standards than those required by the 1979 law. Such a policy might be called the Revised New Source Performance Standard with a 40-year age limit (RNSPS-40). By this standard, all older plants would be replaced by 2020 with new ones which could meet a RNSPS of about 0.1 pound sulfur dioxide per million Btu (equivalent to 99 percent reduction in emissions).

Taking into account the age of the current utility fleet of generating plants and applying RNSPS-40, the sulfur dioxide emissions would drop continually from the present. By the year 2000, they would be reduced by about four million tons per year, by 2010 about nine million tons, and by 2020 about 14 million tons, compared to 10 million tons for the CAA.

The *net cost* to society of the RNSPS-40 is close to zero, since the new plants cost no more than those meeting the current 1979 NSPS, yet virtually eliminate the sulfur dioxide emissions. By contrast, the 1990 CAA strategy will cost about $100 billion to retrofit and operate the old plants before they are retired.

Since negligible, or only modest, environmental effects exist as a result of historical concentrations of acidity of rain in the most heavily impacted areas of the United States, and no worsening of the situation is expected in the next half century even without additional regulation, there is no reason for a "crash" strategy such as is built into the 1990 Clean Air Act.

Some variation of the RNSPS-40 strategy would be clearly superior to the 1990 CAA crash-retrofit strategy, as it could save on the order of $100 billion, produce a better environmental result, would make more efficient use of society's capital, would produce less solid waste, nitrogen oxides, and, by improving the thermal efficiency of our power generating plants, would also substantially reduce carbon dioxide emissions.

The Clean Air Act Must Be Revised

Since the first phase of the 1990 CAA strategy requires removal of five million tons of sulfur dioxide, which will be done at relatively low cost by fuel switching, replacement of the least efficient, oldest, and smallest plants by gas turbines, and maximizing the use of low or zero emission (i.e., nuclear or hydroelectric power) plants, there is time to revise the 1990 CAA retrofit strategy to take advantage of the obvious benefits of a strategy involving deployment of advanced technology in new plants on a stretched timescale. Let us hope that such a reassessment will be undertaken by the administration and urged upon Congress as a new, more enlightened amendment to the Clean Air Act.

119

"Free market environmentalism moves us in the direction of a bargaining process between the polluters and the receptors of pollution."

Market Incentives Are Necessary to Reduce Acid Rain

Terry L. Anderson and Donald R. Leal

Some experts believe that acid rain and other types of pollution are difficult to control because no one "owns" the air and water and consequently no one is harmed economically by damage to these natural resources. In the following viewpoint, excerpted from their book *Free Market Environmentalism*, Terry L. Anderson and Donald R. Leal agree with this analysis and argue that free market incentives that allow companies to purchase and sell their pollution rights would be an inexpensive, effective way to reduce acid rain. Anderson is a professor of economics at Montana State University in Bozeman and a senior economist at the Pacific Research Institute public policy think tank in San Francisco. Leal is a research associate at the institute.

As you read, consider the following questions:

1. Why do the authors believe that current efforts to reduce sulfur dioxide emissions will not reduce acid rain?
2. What are "tradeable pollution permits" and how would they work, according to Anderson and Leal?
3. What example do the authors give to show how market incentives could combat acid rain?

Reprinted from: *Free Market Environmentalism* by Terry L. Anderson and Donald R. Leal, 1991, by permission of Westview Press, Boulder, Colorado.

Acid rain . . . is likely to produce [what S. Fred Singer called] "a billion-dollar solution for a million-dollar problem." According to one ten-year study, however, the effects of acid rain are not as widespread as some have claimed. The National Acid Precipitation Assessment Program (NAPAP) found that "a firm causal link has proved to be elusive" between acid rain and areas where forests have been dying; natural stresses seem to be the primary causes. The only exception is that acid rain "may to a small degree reduce the frost hardiness of red spruce in a narrow elevational band in the Northeast." Researchers have also shown that agricultural crops are sensitive to ozone but not to acid rain; in fact, acid rain may even contribute to soil fertility. Acid rain's effect on building materials also has been difficult to quantify, but it is doubtful that it has had much effect. Neither is there solid evidence of acid rain causing adverse health effects. There is evidence that acid rain causes some deterioration in visibility and acidification of lakes in New York's Adirondack Mountains, Pennsylvania's Pocono Mountains, and in Michigan's Upper Peninsula, but there is other evidence that local geology, land use, and soil drainage may be the cause of the high lake acidity.

The NAPAP study found that efforts to drastically reduce SO_2 [sulfur dioxide] emissions to control acid rain are not well founded, because "percentage reductions in emissions may not result in similar percentage reductions in [acid] depositions." Between 1972, when SO_2 emissions peaked, and 1988, emissions decreased by 25 percent. According to the director of the NAPAP study, however, "no apparent trend in the acidity of rainfall has been detected."

Appeal of Market Approach

Even though there is little evidence that acid rain is causing widespread problems and that reducing SO_2 emissions can have a significant impact on acid rain, the Bush administration proposed reducing SO_2 emissions by 10 million tons (from the 1980 base year level). The cost of this reduction has been estimated to be from $4 billion to $7 billion per year over the next twenty years. To minimize the costs, there appears to be increasing sympathy with the "market-like" approach of establishing emission standards and allowing plants to trade their allowances. This would be a big improvement over "best available technology" regulations, because greater flexibility is allowed in achieving reductions and lowers costs by allowing the lowest-cost plants to sell their emission permits and reduce emissions. Just as individual, transferable quotas allow the government to set the total catch allowed from a fishery and then let the market decide how and by whom the catch will be taken, tradeable pollution permits offer a market-based approach to air pollution. By making tradeable pollution permits the centerpiece of his attack on acid rain, President Bush acknowledged that incentives are important. For economists who have advocated more efficiency in controlling pollution, Bush's approach is a welcome alternative to more inefficient regulations. [As Robert W. Hahn stated:]

> This market approach would induce firms with low-cost pollution control technologies to clean up more and would thus reduce the overall cost of achieving environmental quality goals by about 50 percent, or over $13 billion, compared with traditional command-and-control approaches, which specify the precise technology that firms must use.

As Daniel Dudek, economist for the Environmental Defense Fund, put it, "The beauty of this approach is that it provides environmental performance without great bloodletting in the economy." Tradeable pollution permits are even supported by some environmentally minded politicians, such as Senator Timothy Wirth (D-Colorado), who said, "We're not going to be able to make a dent in environmental problems unless we can harness the forces of the marketplace.". . .

COST OF DEACIDIFYING LAKES

REGION	ACRES OF ACID LAKE	Annual Cost of Liming	
		BY HELICOPTER	BY BOAT
Adirondacks	4,846	$1,211,500	$242,300
Southern New England	5,669	1,417,200	283,400
Central New England	480	120,000	24,000
TOTAL NORTHEAST	12,496	3,124,000	625,000
Upper Midwest	2,628	657,000	131,000
TOTAL IMPACT AREA	**15,124**	**$3,781,000**	**$756,000**

Source: NAPAP Interim Assessment 1987 Living Lakes Data.

Government has an important role to play in this free market solution. Just as states registered cattle brands and prosecuted rustlers, the government could move us in the direction of free market environmentalism if it would register pollutants, monitor the flow of pollutants in the atmosphere, and enforce liability for damages.

It would be possible to identify power plants that are most responsible for acid rain problems in the Northeast. With the sources of pollutants identified, polluters could be forced to pay for the damages they cause. If SO_2 pollution affects visibility, then property values will reflect the damages, thus giving property owners the basis for seeking damages or injunctions. In the case of surface water acidity, establishing private rights to water would give the owners similar standing in courts. Where the damages are localized and identifiable, expensive, nationwide solutions become unnecessary. For example, the NAPAP assessment identified approximately 2 percent of total lake area in the Northeast and Midwest as having a pH of 5 or less. This threshold is important because field observations show that most species of fish tolerate pH levels above 5.5, but relatively few species can sustain populations in acidic water with a pH below 5. According to the NAPAP study, lakes with pH of 5 or less could be neutralized by dumping lime into them from helicopters every year. The annual cost would be less than $4 million and could be reduced to less than $800,000 if boats were used. This is about one-tenth of 1 percent of the lowest estimated annual cost required in the Bush administration's proposal to reduce SO_2 emissions. If polluters were liable to property owners for the damages they caused, they would have the incentive to undertake their own deacidification progams and minimize the costs.

No Easy Solution

At this point, we must emphasize that the property rights approach offers no panacea. Property rights are costly to define and enforce, but these costs are a function of the value of the resource in question and the technology. There is no more guarantee that property rights will evolve than there is that regulatory solutions will achieve the optimal level of pollution. The difference between the two approaches is that free market environmentalism moves us in the direction of a bargaining process between the polluters and the receptors of pollution.

"Polluters will feel they have carte blanche to raise the flag of 'market incentives' whenever they want to avoid or weaken environmental requirements."

Market Incentives May Not Reduce Acid Rain

Claude Engle and Hawley Truax

While many have touted market incentives as an effective way to reduce acid rain, such incentives also pose problems. In the following viewpoint, Claude Engle and Hawley Truax express some of the concerns environmentalists have about bringing market influences into environmental issues. The authors conclude that industry will be motivated by profit, not by concern for the environment, and will also come to believe it has the right to pollute at certain levels. Engle writes on environmental issues. Truax is an editor for *Environmental Action*, a bimonthly magazine.

As you read, consider the following questions:

1. How are market influences supposed to reduce acid rain, according to the authors?
2. Why will market-based efforts at reducing acid rain be difficult to enforce, in the authors' opinion?
3. Why won't market incentives be effective at controlling pollution by public utilities, according to Engle and Truax?

Reprinted, with permission, from Claude Engle and Hawley Truax, "The Carrot or the Stick?" *Environmental Action*, May/June 1990.

These days, phrases like "using the market," "market-based approach," and "market incentives" are cropping up so often in Washington environmental circles that they are beginning to seem positively trendy.

It's not that the idea of harnessing market forces to protect the environment is a new one. It's been floating around in the academic community for decades. In a general sense, we already rely on market forces to encourage environmentally responsible behavior. And regulators have specifically used a market approach—in isolated cases—with some success.

But, a rash of new ideas have moved off the drawing boards of academics and environmental planners and into the halls of the White House and Congress. . . .

Getting beyond the buzz phrases to understand market approaches can be difficult. The world of market analysis is a world of economists, lawyers and long-term planners whose jargon-filled position papers do not translate readily to the layperson.

At least some of the roots of the market-oriented approach date back to the 1930s and the work of A.C. Pigou, an economist at Cambridge University in England. Pigou observed that producers and consumers who pollute the environment do not generally pay for their pollution—even though they may harm others or cause others (or society) to incur the costs of clean up.

Market approaches are about "internalizing" those costs—forcing industry to take responsibility for the true environmental toll of its actions. As one market-oriented environmentalist puts it, "We must set up the rules of the game so that companies' own self-interest lies in safeguarding the environment."

At some level, most existing approaches to environmental protection—from government fines to citizen lawsuits to publicity campaigns to boycotts—aim to change polluter behavior through adverse financial impact. Today's market-oriented enthusiasts believe that continually threatening industry is not the most effective means of achieving environmental protection. They are tired of wielding sticks, and propose proffering some carrots instead.

Environmentalists Must Consider Industry's Interests

In a November 1986 op-ed for the *Wall Street Journal*, the new director of the Environmental Defense Fund (EDF), Frederic Krupp, argued that it is no longer sufficient for environmentalists to oppose pollution. Krupp called for a new generation of environmental advocates who carefully consider the impact of regulation on industry, taking into account everything from economic growth and jobs to taxpayer and stockholder interests.

As described by Krupp, these "third stage" environmentalists recognize that at the bottom of most environmental problems (from pesticides to dams) are legitimate social needs, and that one can't just oppose the problem without finding a way to meet the need.

Environmentalists are hiking down a very slippery slope when they start focusing on the needs of industry, objects Environmental Action's Clean Air lobbyist Casey Padgett. "It's a question of whether environmental policy should be dictated by the needs of industry or the need to protect our citizens' health," says Padgett. "Pollution trading emphasizes saving industry money over saving human lives.". . .

Pollution "Credits"

The emissions trading concept dates back to 1974 when EPA [Environmental Protection Agency] began to allow firms that reduced their pollution emissions below the level required by law at one site, to accrue "credits" that could be used against excessive emissions elsewhere. EPA also allowed polluters to pursue a "bubble" approach, through which a plant could cut emissions from several large smokestacks in place of abating emissions from hundreds of small, difficult-to-control vents or valves.

In 1976, the trading concept was expanded in California when a regional EPA official allowed companies to establish new emissions sources in heavily polluted, "non-attainment" areas if those air pollutants were offset at another site.

The 1990 acid rain amendment to the Clean Air Act departs from previous pollution trading in that it grants utilities a "right" to pollute at certain levels. Every ton of pollution that a firm manages to cut beyond its assigned limit would become a marketable asset—a credit—to be banked for expansion at some later time or sold to the highest bidder. Thus, rather than simply a regulatory burden, pollution control becomes a profit opportunity.

Under the acid rain program, the emissions trading market would be far more complicated than current options, with features like emission-credit banking, out-of-state trading, annual growth auctions for new power generators, and an "opt-in" provision to let companies not covered by the program get into the new lucrative trading scheme.

Flexibility is a key feature of the acid rain legislation. Utilities are free to decide how they will meet reduced averages—by installing scrubbers, burning alternative fuels or lower sulfur coal, encouraging energy conservation, building cleaner units or buying pollution permits from another plant. Advocates believe that this decision will be made most prudently and efficiently by companies themselves.

The legislation outlines a two-phase, 10 million ton reduction in SO_2 [sulfur dioxide] emissions and a two million ton cut in NO_x [nitrogen-oxygen compounds] emissions. According to EPA analyses, the emissions trading and added flexibility of this approach could reduce the annual cost of acid rain control by 50 percent, with no compromise in environmental goals.

Benefits to Industry

As expected, industry response to the trading concept has been favorable. Pennsylvania Electric's Al Slowik notes that if a scrubber module breaks down, a utility can compensate by purchasing pollution credits rather than having to invest in back-up scrubbers.

On the flip side, some environmentalists criticize the strategy for failing to require the best reductions possible given current pollution control technology.

FUNNY... HE NEVER MENTIONED IT WAS GOING TO BE <u>ACID</u> RAIN.

© Mike Peters. Reprinted with permission.

"Pollution trading systems inherently do not set the best available standards," points out EA's Padgett, "because if they did polluters couldn't surpass reduction requirements and gain credits to sell to other facilities."

Enforcement is another concern. If EPA is already overburdened, how can the agency possibly handle the complicated new role of monitoring all pollution credits? Under the proposed system, to check whether one utility is complying with the Clean Air Act, EPA would have to check that utility's own emissions, as well as the emissions of every utility with which it had traded credits. It's like the AIDS warning—when you have sex with one person, you have to think about all their previous partners, and all their previous partners, and so on. . . .

In an internal memo to Rep. John Dingell (D-Mich.), chair of the House Energy and Commerce Committee, staffer Michael Woo questions whether the entire basis of the credit trading scheme is sound, at least when applied to the utility industry.

The emissions trading approach assumes that utilities will have an economic incentive to create and sell pollution credits. But utilities are regulated monopolies, and their ability to generate unlimited profits is restricted. They do not have the same profit motive to clean up beyond required levels that one might find in a less regulated sector.

Woo goes on to question whether utilities that did pursue further reductions would be willing to sell their credits. Woo points out that the utility industry is traditionally conservative, and that many companies might prefer to bank credits (or "hoard" them, as some critics prefer to put it) against future growth opportunities. State public utility commissions might adopt the same reasoning, Woo notes, blocking utilities from trading their credits out of states so that the state would have a "pollution margin" for future economic growth.

Legalized Poisoning

It's not surprising that the Bush administration cast its lot with the emissions trading scheme. The approach was tailor-made for a president who campaigned as an environmentalist—but had a long history of opposing environmental regulations.

Sierra Club's Dan Becker, who has worked on Clean Air for years, concludes: "The Senate has placed its trust in an untested market-based approach, assuming that industry and the administration will act in good faith, and that there will be a perfect market in an industry where there is none.". . .

EA's Casey Padgett criticizes the National Clean Air Coalition for its silence on the emissions trading proposal. "Over the many years of working on this bill," says Padgett, "the Clean Air Coalition has become somewhat parochial, even myopic, in its vision. The coalition sometimes fails to look at the big picture and the concerns of citizens across the country. It's a classic inside-the-beltway response, dictated by a sense of what is possible, what is reasonable to get done, given today's political realities."

The very idea that industry has a right to pollute at certain levels leaves a bad taste in the mouth of many environmentalists. "Laws which legalize poisoning are wrong," states Richard Grossman, publisher of the *Wrenching Debate Gazette.*

"You mean paying to pollute?" asks Dr. Barry Commoner, "I think the whole notion is an abomination."

Grassroots environmental advocates, historically skeptical of EPA's role as protector of the people, are likely to be especially concerned by the trading proposal. The acid rain law gives the EPA administrator power to oversee all pollution credit transactions; and does not require public hearings, public comment opportunities or subject these decisions to judicial review. . . .

Even if we don't see adverse effects from this acid rain legislation, EA's Padgett worries that it sets a bad precedent. "I can see it already," says Padgett, "polluters will feel they have carte blanche to raise the flag of 'market incentives' whenever they want to avoid or weaken environmental requirements."

Global Pollution Trading

Pollution trading is already rearing its head in other areas. Bills promoting tradeable recycling credits have been introduced. . . . And an international trading scheme has even been developed to fight global warming.

"EDF has proposed emissions trading for acid rain, where it probably won't work," warns Sierra's Dan Becker. "Now—giddy with success—they are pushing for a similar program to stem global warming, where it certainly won't work. How do you enforce an agreement where Brazil would preserve its rain forest, if Pakistan limits its population growth?"

Periodical Bibliography

The following articles have been selected to supplement the diverse views presented in this chapter.

Acid Precipitation Digest	Entire periodical on acid rain. Available from Air Resources Information Clearinghouse, 46 Prince St., Rochester, NY 14607.
William Anderson	"Acid Test," *Reason*, January 1992.
Timothy Beardsley	"Acid Test: A Mammoth Assessment Fails to Find All the Answers," *Scientific American*, April 1990.
Derek Burney	"Canada and the United States in a Global Context," *Vital Speeches of the Day*, November 1, 1989.
John E. Carroll	"The Acid Challenge to Security," *The Bulletin of the Atomic Scientists*, October 1989.
Environment	"Pouring Forth on Acid Rain," March 1990.
John Flynn	"Forests Without Trees," *The Amicus Journal*, Winter 1991.
Leen Hordijk	"A Model Approach to Acid Rain," *Environment*, March 1988.
Edward C. Krug	"The Corrosion of Science," *Liberty*, March 1992. Available from Liberty Publishing, PO Box 1167, Port Townsend, WA 98368.
Laurence J. Kulp	"Acid Rain: Causes, Effects, and Control," *Regulation*, Winter 1990. Available from Circulation Dept., Cato Institute, 224 Second St. SE, Washington, DC 20003.
Sheryl Lechner	"Liming Acid Lakes," *Audubon*, May/June 1992.
Robert W. Lee	"The Theory That's All Wet," *The New American*, June 1, 1992. Available from 770 Westhill Blvd., Appleton, WI 54915.
Leslie Roberts	"Learning from an Acid Rain Program," *Science*, March 15, 1991.
D.W. Schindler	"Effects of Acid Rain on Freshwater Ecosystems," *Science*, January 8, 1988.
Daniel Seligman	"Our Government Fails an Acid Test," *Fortune*, February 11, 1991.

How Serious a Problem Is Ocean Pollution?

Chapter Preface

The earth's oceans are vast. The Pacific Ocean alone covers more than 100 million square miles and is almost five times larger than Africa. Because of the immense size of the oceans, humans have unhesitatingly used them as dumping grounds for human waste, chemical waste, garbage, and toxins, believing that the oceans would be able to absorb anything dumped into them with little harm.

The oceans are resilient. Yet, many environmentalists believe humans are pushing the bounds of what the oceans can accept. In one year alone, the major industrial nations produced more than nine billion tons of solid waste, 300 million tons of which was hazardous. Much of this waste ended up in the oceans. Pollution that poisons marine life is killing off some species and causing irreparable harm to others. Garbage snares and kills fish, birds, and sea mammals.

Toxic chemicals, plastic, and other vestiges of modern life are affecting the oceans in ways humans never anticipated or pondered. As writer and environmentalist Wayne Ellwood states, "The sea, the ancient symbol of timelessness, continuity and fecundity, is being overwhelmed by the breathtaking pace of modern life. Space-age technology, Third World poverty and old-fashioned greed have suddenly combined to form the first serious threat to the oceans since creation."

While not all experts believe ocean pollution is as serious a problem as Ellwood states, they do agree that a problem exists and must be addressed. The authors in the following chapter present their views on what measures, if any, should be taken to reduce ocean pollution.

"Oil has . . . become a key element in our lifestyle. Today, though, its benefits can be offset, if not overtaken, by its rising environmental price."

Oil Spills Threaten the Oceans

Wesley Marx

"Never before have the global shore and our oceans been so burdened by such a hideous hodgepodge of our liquid and solid castaways," environmentalist Wesley Marx states in his book *The Frail Ocean*. In the following viewpoint, excerpted from the book, Marx explains how oil is one of the most damaging of humankind's "liquid castaways." Oil spills kill birds, otters, and other marine life, and coat coastlines with a thick, gooey film of pollution. Marx concludes that the most effective way to reduce oil spills is to end America's dependence on oil.

As you read, consider the following questions:

1. What does Marx mean when he says that "for the oil industry, the coastal zone is an extended workplace"?
2. What evidence does the author give to show that efforts to clean up spills are inadequate?
3. How does the author connect America's use of oil to global warming?

Reprinted with permission from *The Frail Ocean* © 1991 by Wesley Marx. Published by The Globe Pequot Press, Inc., Old Saybrook, CT.

The sea winds were blowing onshore, cooling off a million weekend bathers escaping the hot August heat. But this breezy salvation for a sweltering southern California bothered the Coast Guard official. "You don't want these winds when a tanker spills oil," he explained to me. "With winds like this, the skimmers are useless and the spill gets legs, real long legs." The fallback plan for this, I learned, would be to boom off three major ports, call off naval maneuvers, move some sea otters to onshore safety, and mobilize a work crew of 5,000 to hand-clean some 400 miles of the world's most photogenic coastline.

That high-tech, high-flying California could be momentarily brought down on its economic knees by the long reach of spilled oil is but one example of how coastal regions find themselves entangled in the strengths and weaknesses of one industrial enterprise. Oil has fueled the industrial revolution and become a key element in our life-style. Today, though, its benefits can be offset, if not overtaken, by its rising environmental price for those who live and work along the coastal rim.

The New Frontier

For the oil industry, the coastal zone is an extended workplace. Here are the ports to receive oil, the refineries to process it, the tank farms to store it, the pipelines to ship it inland and keep our cars and trucks rolling. Here, too, begin the sea-lanes to ship oil around the world. And here begins the new "frontier"—the offshore oil fields to prolong our hydrocarbon existence as onshore reserves run out.

Today, the ports of Los Angeles, San Francisco, and New York each host about 1,000 tanker visits a year. Some 4,000 oil platforms dot the new frontier, from the chilly waters of Alaska to the humid Gulf of Mexico. Three hundred additional artificial islands pump more oil. In the Gulf of Mexico, the busiest marine frontier, some 25,000 kilometers of oil pipelines criss-cross the seabed and coastal wetlands.

And that's only a dress rehearsal for the future. The oil industry wants to open up such new frontier areas as Georges Banks off Massachusetts, the waters off Washington and Oregon, and, in Alaska, the Beaufort and Bering seas and the Arctic National Wildlife Refuge. From Norway to China, other nations rush to open up their frontiers, often in joint ventures with U.S. oil firms, the pioneers and leaders in offshore oil technology. "We need it all," explained a Unocal executive eager to explore some thirty-nine new offshore tracts along California's Central Coast. "That's what we need to sustain our way of life."

For most of this century, coastal regions have been willing to accommodate such marine visions. For Louisiana, Texas, and Alaska, offshore oil royalties can reduce or eliminate the need for state income taxes or property taxes. For Uncle Sam, oil revenues from the outer continental shelf (the area beyond state jurisdiction) are second only to income taxes as a revenue source.

There were some early omens that the rush into the marine frontier could backfire. In 1967, despite a clear day, calm waters, high tide, excellent charts, a warning flare from a lighthouse ship, and a sterling 100A1 rating from Lloyd's insurers, the *Torrey Canyon* still slammed into Seven Stones Reef to become a historic shipwreck. The cargo of the tanker was a liquid one, totaling thirty-six million gallons, ordinarily a raindrop in the vast solution of the ocean. But the ocean cannot absorb oil very efficiently. Within three days, slicks the color of melted chocolate sprawled over a hundred square miles of ocean, a moving quagmire that ensnared seabirds by the thousands. The slicks, with their cargo of flightless birds, rolled up on the golden beaches of Cornwall and the pink granite coast of Brittany. As no coastal storm could ever do, this oil-smeared sea incapacitated the coasts of two nations and defied cleanup efforts.

In 1969, another style of oil spill made its debut, the offshore oil blowout that can coat 800 square miles of nearshore and smear thirty miles of beach, as happened in the Unocal blowout off Santa Barbara, California. Despite such troublesome omens, coastal regions continued to accept more development on the burgeoning marine frontier. The oil industry that had the expertise to build supertankers longer than football fields and oil platforms taller than the Empire State Building said it would develop the technology to clean up the next spill. Regulatory agencies told the oil industry to prepare spill contingency plans. Some critics urged that the thin-skinned tankers be equipped with double hulls to reduce the risk of spills from the next collision. Such urgings were largely ignored.

A High Price to Pay

But the specter of spills and of inadequate or tardy control efforts persisted. The 1978 *Amoco Cadiz* spill off France and the 1979 Ixtoc-I blowout in Mexico that reached as far north as Texas reaffirmed the limits of relying on impromptu cleanups. Were damaging spills really an unavoidable price that coastal regions would have to learn to accept?

In 1989, the spill that wasn't supposed to happen did happen. The *Exxon Valdez*, now named *Exxon Mediterranean*, ran into Bligh Reef in Alaska's Prince William Sound and spilled eleven million gallons of Arctic crude. This spill could not be blamed on the prototype "rust bucket" tanker able to skimp on safety by being flagged in Liberia. This was a vessel owned and operated by the largest oil company in the United States and subject to regulation by Alaska and the United States. Some 1,200 miles of shore would receive an oily absolution. About 33,000 seabirds would be killed. So would 1,000 sea otters. The cleanup technology for such a large spill simply wasn't there.

Dick Wright reprinted by permission of UFS, Inc.

Or, for that matter, anywhere. In March 1990, the *American Tanker* punctured its hull with its anchor while preparing to unload more Alaskan crude. This time the spill recipient would be the coastline of Orange County, California. The skimmers materialized faster than at Valdez, and the winds were initially cooperative. The amount of oil spilled—400,000 gallons—was much less than that from the *Valdez*. Yet only 20 percent would be recovered at sea. Too much wound up on birds—some 700 died—and along a fifteen-mile stretch of sandy beach, one of the busiest and most popular of all sandy shores in the world. This stretch of beach had to close down for a month as the shores were hand-cleaned, oil glob by oil emulsion. As Coast Guard Commandant Admiral Paul Yost told local reporters, "I'm not satisfied with the skimming capability we have in the United States—especially the high seas capability. We don't have enough." If an industrial nation like the United States is so defenseless, you can imagine where this leaves coastal regions like the Caribbean, exposed to extensive tanker traffic.

Ineffective Attempts to Clean Up Oil

The 20 percent recovery rate, while not adequate to protect either wildlife or the beaches, was a smash performance compared with most efforts at spill control. According to a 1990 Office of Technology Assessment study, booms and skimmers can recover only about 10 percent of oil spilled. Moreover, this technology works only under limited conditions. Based on actual tests, the California Coastal Commission found that skimmers and other cleanup equipment are not effective in waves higher than six feet or in currents of more than one knot—conditions that can prevail off southern California 25 percent of the time and in central and northern California 50 to 80 percent of the time. Use of chemical dispersants to "sink" spills can create toxic problems. Burning of spills can be limited by weather and the need to initiate burning before the slick spreads too thinly. Thus, two decades after the *Torrey Canyon* and Santa Barbara spills and despite the repeated assurances of the oil industry and its regulators, coastal regions still find themselves hostage to the shortcomings of marine oil development. . . .

To reduce the demand for imported oil and the risks of more tanker spills, the oil industry has an answer: Accelerate the oil leasing of offshore America. To coastal states, however, this idea seems to be a case of going out of the frying pan and into the fire. Spills from oil platforms can be just as hard to control as those from tankers. And the promise of replacing tankers with platforms can, like spill control, be illusory. In deeper-water areas, platform producers may find it cheaper to tanker their crude rather than pipe it onshore. As a result, some offshore leases could *increase* tanker traffic and the risk of spills. In a 1989 federal impact report, coastal officials in central California learned that one proposed lease sale would increase tanker traffic by 41 percent, or 400 more tanker transits per year at peak production. At least four major accidents could be expected, including a tanker spill, a platform spill, and at least two serious pipeline leaks. This seems like a curious way to save our seas from slips by foreign tankers. . . .

High Settlements Help Restore Habitat

Coastal states can raise the ante for repeated spills, large or small. In 1988, a tank owned by Shell Oil leaked, spilling oil into coastal wetlands and San Francisco Bay. Dikes to contain such spills were built too low. While not a big spill, the event still involved enough oil to damage wetland habitat, injure birds, and interrupt fishing, birding, and boating. By ascertaining the value of lost wildlife and lost opportunities in coastal activities and adding this amount to cleanup costs, California Attorney General John Van De Kamp, working with federal resources agencies, secured a $20 million settlement from Shell, much higher than the normal assessment for spills larger in size and impact. This settlement will enable California to restore degraded wetland habitat to compensate for the spill impact and for interruption of coastal activities. In 1990, Congress directed the National Oceanographic and Atmospheric Administration to upgrade the federal government's ability to recover such damages and implement restoration plans.

Through their congressional delegations, coastal states can temper the federal ardor for offshore oil leases. After vigorous lobbying by coastal legislators including California's Senator-turned-Governor Peter Wilson, President Bush agreed to a ten-year delay in new leases off much of California and all of southwestern Florida, Washington, Oregon, and New England. . . . Coastal states would like this pledge to be enacted as law.

At the same time, coastal states have been stepping up their lobbying for federal conservation initiatives. An increase in federal auto fuel efficiency standards of just two more miles of gas per gallon could save more oil than the Arctic National Wildlife Refuge could produce.

Oil and Global Warming

If the long-standing hazards of marine oil development don't drive home the need for such energy alternatives, a newer hazard may. Global warming, by inducing rising sea levels, may eventually threaten Miami and other low-lying coastal regions. A major cause of global warming, carbon dioxide (CO_2) emissions, is the burning of fossil fuels. Coastal states that are being urged to expedite offshore oil leasing are in effect being asked to play host to the very energy source that could drown their beaches, mangrove forests, coral reefs, and cities, inch by rising inch of sea level. . . .

In the United States, coastal states will need to play an increasing role in shaping a prudent federal response to such a critical issue. Coastal legislators like Senate Majority Leader George Mitchell (D.-Maine) support the need for a more farsighted response. . . . The United States and other industrial nations may eventually be able to gain credits for required CO_2 emission cuts by transferring renewable and energy-efficient technologies to developing nations. By helping to cultivate such energy options, coastal states like California and Hawaii have demonstrated that energy policy need not be on a collision course with a safe environment.

"The chemicals contained in petroleum have long been part of the marine environment, and physical impacts are likely to be temporary."

The Threat Posed by Oil Spills Is Exaggerated

James E. Mielke

Major oil spills receive extensive media coverage. Photos of oil-covered birds and dead fish cover the front pages of newspapers. These dramatic images lead the public to believe that oil spills are catastrophic to the environment, James E. Mielke states in the following viewpoint. He asserts, however, that nature is in fact only temporarily affected by oil spills, and that they cause little if any long-term damage to the oceans. Mielke is a specialist in marine and earth sciences with the Congressional Research Service for the Library of Congress in Washington, D.C.

As you read, consider the following questions:

1. Why does the author believe that crude oil does not harm the oceans?
2. In the case of the *Argo Merchant* spill, how did the reality differ from the public perception, in Mielke's opinion?
3. What effect do clean-up efforts have on oil spills and on nature, according to the author?

From James E. Mielke, "Oil Spills: Is the Perception Worse than the Reality?" *Forum for Applied Research and Public Policy*, Winter 1991. Reprinted with permission.

Offshore oil spills commonly elicit images of oiled birds, dead fish, large slicks, and massive amounts of sludge washing ashore to despoil a scenic beach or pristine environment.

These were the images portrayed for three months after the *Exxon Valdez* spill. Some commentators proclaimed it the greatest ecological disaster of all time from which it would take Alaska's Prince William Sound at least 50 to 100 years to recover. Fears were raised that the sound's salmon and herring fisheries would be devastated.

Yet, field observations conducted in 1990 show that the environment in the sound and gulf has undergone a robust recovery. The 1990 catch of 40 million pink salmon in Prince William Sound set a record, far eclipsing the previous record harvest of 29 million.

Perceptions Do Not Match Reality

An oil spill has two lives. One is the short-term life generated by human interest, including that of the media, nearby residents, state and local governments, and environmental groups. The other life is the biogeochemical life cycle of carbon and its compounds in the natural environment.

The former is generally given great attention; the latter rarely is considered outside the technical and scientific literature. Consequently, the perceived impact of an oil spill may be only vaguely related to what ultimately happens to the oil or to the oil's interaction with the affected area. This factor has significant policy implications because decision makers often are influenced by the perceived impacts of events.

Crude oil has always been a natural part of the biosphere. In fact, oil has been common to the oceans for hundreds of millions of years, long before humans. Oil forms largely from the burial and transformation of marine organisms under heat and pressure over geologic time. Most of the oil has not been trapped in reservoirs but has seeped to the surface where it has been decomposed, digested, and recycled.

Many seeps are small, but many are not. Although difficult to quantify, it is estimated that 1.5 million barrels of oil enter the oceans from natural seeps each year, and even this amount may be an order of magnitude too low.

Oil that is spilled or seeps naturally into the ocean is eventually accommodated by physical, chemical, and biological processes. These processes include spreading, evaporation, solution, emulsification, tar lump formation, photochemical oxidation, microbial degradation, organic uptake, and sedimentation and shoreline stranding. Factors specific to each spill influence the effectiveness of these processes and determine the severity of the ecological impact.

Although human intervention can help make a shoreline look clean, it rarely has been effective in removing oil. In fact, improper clean-up methods can be detrimental to the ecological restoration of the area. Historically, an average of less than 4 percent and seldom more than 10 percent of the oil from a large spill has been recovered. . . .

The News Media and Damage Perceptions

Several researchers have probed the media's influence on the public in response to oil spills and other events. For example, investigators studying the Santa Barbara spill concluded that the frequency and nature of reporting an oil spill could be predicted on the basis of the media's geographical proximity to the event. They also showed that an event receives much more coverage at the time of the mishap and comparatively little, nonlocal coverage afterwards.

Initial reporting often focuses on the more "newsworthy" elements, *e.g.*, the threat to the health or environmental values of society. For example, media coverage of medical wastes found on beaches on Long Island and northern New Jersey in July 1988 caused beach scares resulting in more than $1 billion in lost revenues to other resort areas at which no wastes were found. In the case of an oil spill, it takes time to investigate the long-term effects; results often are not available for a year or more. Press coverage of these later results generally is minimal and largely confined to the more scientific literature.

The *Argo Merchant* and the *Amoco Cadiz* are two spills that occurred long enough ago for long-term effects to become apparent and for media attention to subside. The events received extensive media coverage and are still viewed by many as major environmental catastrophes. In fact, the environmental damage and socioeconomic consequences were relatively modest and, as far as can be determined, of relatively short duration.

On December 15, 1976, the Liberian-registered tanker, *Argo Merchant*, grounded on the Nantucket Shoals off Massachusetts. Heavy seas caused the ship to break up, releasing 183,000 barrels of No. 6 residual fuel oil. Attempts to burn the oil proved unsuccessful. The heavy oil formed a large slick, which eventually moved out to sea and dispersed. The estimated response costs of the accident were $2.7 million.

In a study of media coverage, researchers found that public perceptions of local damages presented an interesting and intriguing paradox. Post-spill investigators generally agree that economic damages were minimal (aside from the ship and cargo). Within a year, the area's economy—largely dependent on tourism, water transportation, and commercial fishing—generally reported robust trade. Fortunately, pollution damage also

141

was minimal. There was little evidence of impact on marine bird populations off the New England coast.

At the time of the accident, Environmental Protection Agency Administrator Russell E. Train described the event as "the biggest oil-spill disaster on the American coast in our history." Massachusetts governor Michael S. Dukakis asked President Ford to declare southeastern Massachusetts a disaster area that would qualify it for federal relief funds. Television coverage featured the visual image of the grounded tanker and the subsequent oil slick. As the slick broke up and moved out to sea, television coverage subsided.

What Happens When Oil Spills

When oil is released by a spill or a natural seep, it immediately undergoes a series of natural processes which disperse, decompose, and recycle it. Such processes as evaporation, emulsification, and biodegradation play a larger role in cleaning up the oil in the marine environment than do massive human cleanups.

The CRS [Congressional Research Service] review of past spills indicates that most of the ecological impact occurs at the time of the spill or within a few months. After that, most of the oil has decomposed chemically to the point where it is no longer harmful. Unfortunately, the spill is in the news during that initial period, and this period heavily influences public perceptions. The natural recovery from the spill—and the investigations that confirm it—attract little notice in the popular press; typically, they are reported only in the scientific literature, usually two to five years later.

Donald R. Leal and Michael D. Copeland, *PERC Viewpoints*, April 1991.

While a complete assessment of the environmental damage is impossible to obtain, there seems to be scientific consensus that classifying the incident as an ecological catastrophe has no factual basis.

Researchers who conducted a survey of area residents approximately one year after the accident found that substantially more than half still believed that the *Argo Merchant* spill had caused significant economic or ecological damage. An analysis of press coverage showed that it had shifted from an initial position of little or modest damage to one of catastrophe or major disaster, returning to a position of modest or no damage when the oil moved out to sea. This suggests that once the press portrays the possibility, or existence, of substantial damages, a subsequent withdrawal of such claims does not alter the perceptions of extensive damage held by a large portion of the population. . . .

An oil spill can be devastating. However, past spills have not been long-lived events. The longest residence time that spilled oil has had in the marine and coastal environment has generally been less than a decade—and often much less than that. The major ecological impact has come at the time of the spill or within the first few months. Weathered crude oil is less toxic than fresh oil. Beyond a few months, most oil has been reduced to tarry residues or has been chemically detectable in sediments and resident organisms. These residuals may be of scientific interest but have proven to be rather insignificant in terms of ecological impact.

Citizen Concern

Public impressions of socioeconomic and environmental damage and citizen concerns over ecological impacts have lasted much longer. The life span of the media coverage has been shorter than the spill's major ecological impact but probably of greater significance. With the possible exception of special environments, predictions of long-term effects have been largely unsubstantiated. There has been no evidence of irrevocable damage to marine resources on a broad scale to justify the allegations of unknown but significant long-term effects.

The short-term impact of a major spill can be devastating to the organisms in the vicinity, including shellfish, finfish, marine mammals, and waterfowl. Experience thus far indicates that this has not made a noticeable impact on world population levels of any species. For shellfish, finfish, and waterfowl that are harvested, the mortality from an oil spill, as far as is known, has never come close to approaching the magnitude of the annual harvests. Recolonization of an area temporarily polluted from oil appears to be rapid for most species.

A major short-term impact of a major spill is the visual impression created by an oiled shoreline and featured by media coverage of the event. The media coverage typically includes heartrending scenes of oiled or dead birds and sea life and oiled beaches. The portrayal generally is one of a catastrophe. While not minimizing the effect of an oil spill, it appears that the environmental damage has been less than one would surmise from immediate media coverage.

Nearly one year after the grounding of the *Exxon Valdez*, the city of Valdez issued a press release appealing to the world's press "to avoid repeating errors and myths" in covering the spill anniversary. The press release noted that the loss of wildlife was a small fraction of existing populations and that most of the affected shoreline is remote and beyond the area likely to be seen by tourists. On the other hand, the Alaska Coalition, an environmental group, marked the anniversary by calling on Congress to establish a memorial for the wildlife lost in the accident by declaring the entire Arctic National Wildlife Refuge a wilderness area.

Based on the record of past spills, it also appears that beyond a moderate human effort to clean up an oil spill, nature does a much better job than humans. In fact, in some instances, it appears that the massive clean-up effort delayed the natural ecological restoration of the affected area, although the appearance, particularly of rock and beach areas, may be improved sooner.

This raises the question of whether the cost to society of massive physical clean-up efforts is equal to the social and environmental benefit. In the case of the *Exxon Valdez* spill, the cost of cleanup exceeded $2 billion (far more than had been spent on any previous spill), where most of the affected shoreline is described as "remote and outside the area likely to be seen by seaborne tourists." The unfortunate spill in Prince William Sound, however, will offer an opportunity to study the effects of a large oil spill in a subarctic environment. Whether the effects of the *Exxon Valdez* spill will match the experiences of spills in more temperate environments remains to be seen, but initial reports are encouraging.

Effects of Spills Are Predictable

Oil spills are not new events; many have been studied. Of course, all possible physical, oceanographic, socioeconomic, and environmental effects are not known, and additional scientific study will be valuable. From a public-policy perspective, however, the major socioeconomic and environmental impacts of an oil spill are reasonably well known and, on the basis of that knowledge, the major effects of a future spill should be predictable.

It is reassuring to find broad human concern for the well-being of the seas because, as no other creature before, human beings have the ability to alter a wide range of marine ecosystems dangerously and quickly. Fortunately, however, the oceanic environment is not fragile; in fact, it is resilient. It has evolved through ice ages, global warming, bombardments of cosmic radiation, solar energy fluctuations, massive volcanic eruptions, and collisions of comets and meteors. Mass species extinctions were associated with some of these events, but life forms continued to adapt, evolve, become more complex, and flourish.

Despite short-term attention to the catastrophic nature of major spill events, the chemicals contained in petroleum have long been part of the marine environment, and physical impacts are likely to be temporary in the dynamic natural flux of the coastal environment.

VIEWPOINT

3

"The time has come to dam the spillage of oil."

The Damage Caused by Oil Spills Can Be Prevented

Peter Nulty

Oil spills do not have to be environmental catastrophes, Peter Nulty contends in the following viewpoint. Nulty believes that a few simple measures, such as better-trained tanker crews and sturdier tankers, would prevent oil spills and the environmental damage they cause. Nulty is an associate editor for *Fortune*, a bi-weekly financial magazine.

As you read, consider the following questions:

1. What impact will the increase in oil imports have on the shipping of oil, according to Nulty?
2. What factors determine the damage caused by an oil spill, according to the author?
3. What are the six proposals Nulty makes concerning the prevention of oil spills?

Exxon Valdez. Kill Van Kull. *Mega Borg*. The names of oil spills are beginning to carry the kind of emotional charge usually stored in the names of infamous military defeats: Dunkirk, Pearl Harbor, Tet. One mention and most listeners feel a rush of anger, humiliation, and disappointment. The oil industry is awash with such defeats.

The time has come to dam the spillage of oil. On this much we all agree. After that, the facts about oil spills and what we can do about them are pretty well misunderstood. Two points are paramount: First, the tanker fleet is not spilling more oil than it used to; and second, there's no mystery about what's needed to improve the present record—it's a matter of finding the will.

Despite the impression created by wide coverage of such mishaps as the fire aboard the Norwegian tanker *Mega Borg* off Galveston, Texas, or the *Exxon Valdez*, grounding in Alaska, U.S. Coast Guard records show no clear trend of increase or decrease in the amount of oil being spilled since the early 1970s. The median annual spill rate is just over four million gallons a year.

Like airline disasters, though, monster oil spills seem to come in bunches, and when they do, they skew the record wildly upward. The *Exxon Valdez*, which spilled 10.7 million gallons of crude, accounted for about 80% of the spillage in 1989. A series of spills in New York harbor and the *Mega Borg* incident, which may have put four million gallons into the Gulf of Mexico, made 1990 thoroughly messy. Other bad years include 1975 and 1985, which were even worse than 1989.

Number of Spills Has Decreased

If the plague of accidents represented a new norm, it might justifiably be called a crisis. But nothing in the evidence indicates that is so. The industry's critics are right when they point out that the tanker fleet is aging. Orders for new vessels dropped off in response to reduced demand for oil in the early 1980s. And tanker crews are smaller, replaced in part by electronics. If these changes have resulted in deteriorating seamanship or unseaworthy ships, it doesn't show in the records yet.

On the contrary, the number of pollution-causing tanker accidents recorded by the Coast Guard has fallen by over 50% in the 1980s, suggesting that safety is improving. . . .

Another spate of horrendous spills a few years down the road would also fit the pattern, however, so don't lower the sludge alert banner yet. In fact, run up another one just for emphasis. While chances are that accidents like the *Exxon Valdez* and the *Mega Borg* are not becoming annual events, expect the long-term average rate of spillage to begin climbing—unless even more is done to improve tanker operations.

Oil imports have increased almost 30% since 1986, and they are likely to continue growing. Those imports will arrive in an ever-thickening flow of tanker traffic. Says Sean Connaughton, a marine transportation expert at the American Petroleum Institute, a lobbying organization: "In general, the greater the traffic, the greater the risk."

As imports rise, so will the use of supertankers too large to enter many existing ports. That will result in more "lightering" operations, the transfer of oil to smaller ships for the last part of the journey. The Coast Guard says lightering, which entails some risk of fire or explosion during the transfer, has already doubled since 1988. The *Mega Borg* fire . . . began during lightering.

The U.S. has probably not yet suffered a worldclass, worst-case oil spill disaster. Pray it doesn't. Ranked by size, the *Exxon Valdez* was only the world's 21st-largest spill, according to the *Oil Spill Intelligence Report*, a newsletter in Arlington, Massachusetts. The world's biggest was probably the blowout in 1979 of an offshore Mexican well called Ixtoc 1, which spewed at least 140 million gallons of crude into the Gulf of Mexico. Ixtoc 1 was 15 times larger than the *Valdez* spill and 36 times larger than *Mega Borg*. The environmental impact of Ixtoc was never fully evaluated.

Factors Affecting Level of Damage

Scientists don't know a lot about the damage caused by spills, but one thing they feel sure of: Size is not the most important factor. The type of oil, and weather and sea conditions, count for more. Light oils are more toxic than heavy crudes, although the light varieties evaporate more rapidly. Wind and currents may disperse a spill, which is helpful. Or they may mix it with the sea, thereby poisoning marine life. They may also drive the oil into wetlands and estuaries teeming with wildlife, a worst-case event that for a while seemed possible in the *Mega Borg* accident.

As it happened, the fire was extinguished, saving most of the 38-million-gallon cargo. And most of the oil that spilled burned off or evaporated. Perhaps more significant for the future were the results of the first "bioremediation" experiment conducted on a spill in open waters. Alpha Environmental Inc. of Austin, Texas, spread naturally occurring oil-eating microbes it had gathered from around the world on the *Mega Borg*'s slick. The microbes devoured the oil, in effect eating themselves out of a job and a life. When the oil was gone, they died.

A better approach, of course, is to keep the oil in the ships in the first place. There is surprising unanimity on what steps are needed to do so. What is lacking is the congressional willpower to sweep aside the endless niggling of interest groups intent on gaining some last-minute advantage. Here are some common-sense things to do:

• First, upgrade the traffic-control system run by the Coast Guard. Says Captain Antonio Valdes, vice president of Conoco Shipping Co.: "Europe has tremendous traffic control. The port of Rotterdam is run like an airport. We need more electronic guidance, more buoys, clearer lanes of traffic."

New Tanker Designs Could Prevent Spills

Design	Description and Benefits
Double Hull	The tanker has a double bottom. If the outer layer is breached, the inner layer keeps oil from leaking.
Catamaran	Wide ballast tanks on the sides of the tanker ensure that the oil does not leak if a side collision occurs. A recessed bottom protects the ship from puncturing in a grounding.
Double Tank	Two tanks—an upper and a lower—reduce amount of oil that would leak in a spill.

• Second, train crews better. Roughly 80% of the accidents are caused by human error. An international convention called the Standards for Training and Certification of Watchkeepers sets educational and licensing rules for crew members operating ships in most countries. The Senate has not ratified the treaty, apparently because of pressure from U.S. ship operators who would be required to spend a lot more to train their crews.

• Third, license managers of tanker companies, the owner-operators. Says Arthur McKenzie, founder and director of Tanker Advisory Center Inc., which compiles the safety records of all tankers: "The most important thing about a tanker is who owns it. Do something about the guys in the office." McKenzie suggests that licenses be renewed every few years based in part on the holder's accident and pollution record.

• Fourth, upgrade the fleet with safer tankers. Both houses of Congress have passed bills, calling for double-hulled tankers. The industry generally accepts that double hulls will spill less in an accident than single hulls. But an important principle may be lost. The law should leave open the path to future technologies

148

that may prove superior to double hulls. Congressman Don Young of Alaska says he wants the law to call for "double hulls or better." There just might be some better ideas. Shell International Marine and Mitsubishi have proposed designs that promise significant improvements over double hulls.

• Fifth, establish a clear central authority to direct emergency salvage and cleanup operations. The oil industry is organizing an entity called PIRO (petroleum industry response organization) that plans to set up five spill stations around the country, each with enough equipment—booms, skimmers, and the like—to handle nine-million-gallon spills. The cost: $500 million in the first five years.

PIRO is a good idea, but in an emergency authority over it should lie with the Coast Guard alone. The cleanup of the *Exxon Valdez* spill was slowed by a disagreement between the state of Alaska and the Coast Guard over whether to stabilize the stricken ship first or go after the spreading slick. Moreover, PIRO should be granted immunity from damage suits except in cases of gross negligence. Some members of Congress prefer unlimited liability. But PIRO President Jack Costello fairly asks: "How good would the fire department be if it got sued every time the men broke a door or a window while putting out a fire?"

Establish a Spill Fund

• Finally, a large fund should be established to pay for damages and cleanup, not to let companies off the hook but to be sure the job gets done if an incident involves a company with shallower pockets than Exxon's. There are numerous schemes for how this might be handled. One is to join a set of international protocols. The protocols were vigorously promoted by the U.S. in the early 1980s, then rejected because of opposition in Congress to the concept of limited liability that they embody: $78 million for the owner of a vessel causing a spill. In addition, the protocols provide up to $260 million from a fund created by cargo owners.

These amounts are woefully inadequate. The limit on liability should be high enough to give tanker operators incentive to avoid accidents. Some in Congress favor joining the protocols and then working to enlarge the amounts. Others would create a backup fund of about $1 billion in the U.S., which would be available after the international fund was exhausted.

Whatever solution the lawmakers arrive at should have the following characteristics: The money in reserve should be large, several billion dollars at least. (Exxon has spent more than $2 billion to clean up Prince William Sound and the meter is still running.) This doesn't have to cost consumers very much. A $2 billion fund could be financed by a 5-cents-a-barrel fee on all oil consumed in the U.S. Assuming the cargo owner passes on the cost, roughly one-tenth of a cent would be added to each gallon of fuel. That's both bearable and worth the price.

The issue of spills is coming to a head not because the industry is getting sloppier but because public tolerance is shrinking fast. That is as it should be. Earth's ability to recover from industrial insult is also running down, and only we can recharge it.

"Effective oil recovery is . . . simply impossible."

The Damage Caused by Oil Spills Cannot Be Prevented

Lee Clarke

Oil industry officials, the Coast Guard, and federal and state agencies, among others, have "contingency plans" to help them respond quickly after a major oil spill. Unfortunately, Lee Clarke maintains in the following viewpoint, such plans are worthless. Once a spill has occurred, he argues, nothing can be done to reduce the damage to the environment caused by the oil. Clarke disagrees with those who believe oil spills can be prevented or ameliorated. He concludes that only when the world reduces its dependence on oil will the environmental threat posed by oil spills end. Clarke is a sociology professor at Rutgers University in New Brunswick, New Jersey, and the author of *Acceptable Risk? Making Decisions in a Toxic Environment.*

As you read, consider the following questions:

1. How did the British government respond to the 1967 *Torrey Canyon* oil spill, according to the author?
2. What were the results of the test spill conducted in 1987 by the Canadian Coast Guard, Environment Canada, and the Minerals Management Service, according to Clarke?
3. Why does Clarke believe that, despite their ineffectiveness, contingency plans will continue to be created?

Abridged from Lee Clarke, "Oil-Spill Fantasies," *The Atlantic*, November 1990. Reprinted with permission.

Within hours of the *Exxon Valdez* grounding, in Prince William Sound, officers from the Alaska Department of Environmental Conservation were aboard the stricken vessel. To the extent possible, ADEC officials surveyed the damage and began nudging numerous bureaucracies into action. The night was dark, so officials could not tell how badly damaged the ship was, but they knew the spill would be large. "The oil was several feet deep *on top of the water*," an eyewitness told me (probably with some exaggeration) not long ago. "You could have put a hose in the stuff and sucked it up." One of the first ADEC officials to board the vessel used the ship's radiophone to awaken the terminal superintendent of Alyeska Pipeline Service, the corporation owned by the seven oil companies that oversee the Alaska pipeline. He reported that the spill was "a bad one" and advised that airplanes with oil dispersants be readied immediately. A sense of urgency, even panic, was appropriate, because some of the airplanes and dispersants were in Arizona.

ADEC notified Alyeska first because the consortium bore the greatest organizational and legal responsibility for immediate response to an oil spill in Prince William Sound. The elements of that response are detailed in oil-spill contingency plans, particularly one written by Alyeska and approved by ADEC. Alyeska's contingency plan called, chiefly, for two measures: the use of a containment boom (like a long curtain, partly submerged in the water, which is strung around oil in hopes of controlling it) to hold the leaking oil for later collection with skimmers, and where collection was not possible, the deployment of aircraft with dispersants to dissipate the slick.

As is now common knowledge, both industry and government had major problems implementing Alyeska's contingency plan. Alyeska and Exxon, in particular, have been criticized, with some justification, for responding haltingly or not at all. . . .

"Success" Is All but Impossible

Most public arguments about the Exxon spill have centered on the implementation of contingency plans. However, a crucial point has been overlooked: even under the best of circumstances the response to the *Exxon Valdez* catastrophe would have been a failure. If "success" is defined as recovering 15 percent of the oil—a very modest goal—then neither Alyeska, Exxon, the Coast Guard, ADEC, nor anyone else could possibly have claimed success.

Indeed, *oil has never been successfully contained in a major tankship accident, nor has a recovery operation ever been successful.* Contingency plans are little more than imaginative fictions about what people hope will happen when things go wrong. Contingency plans for major oil spills ("major" meaning more than 100,000 gallons) on the open sea are fantasy documents that organizations use to reassure others that they are in control of potentially uncontrollable situations. These plans, and the promises from experts who promote them, will remain fantastic for the foreseeable future. Although the sophistication of such plans is ever increasing, they are no closer today to spelling out ways to fix oil spills than they were [in 1967], when the first major spill from a supertanker occurred.

The Grounding of the *Torrey Canyon*

In 1967 the *Torrey Canyon*, a 975-foot-long vessel (The *Exxon Valdez*, now the *Exxon Mediterranean*, is 987 feet), ran aground in the English Channel with nearly 35 million gallons of oil on board. Within the first six days 6 million to 12 million gallons of the *Torrey Canyon*'s cargo leaked out and, with assistance from the winds, soon blackened the Cornwall coast. (The Exxon spill was estimated at 11 million gallons.) As in Alaska, a boom to contain the spill was scheduled to arrive soon but didn't. For the first seven days after the stranding, salvors tried to save the ship, to no avail. One salvor died in the attempt. Then the tanker's back broke, whereupon the British government declared war on the wreck. On the tenth day of the crisis eight bombers from the Royal Navy attacked their enemy, dropping 1,000-pound bombs on the crippled vessel in an attempt to burn the oil. Soon the *Torrey Canyon*'s stern was aflame, and Prime Minister Harold Wilson expressed delight with the navy's proficiency. Another attack soon followed, this time by fighter jets dumping 5,000 gallons of aviation fuel on the wreck. By the end of the day eighteen tons of bombs had been dropped on the *Torrey Canyon*. Experts worried that the conflagration might be so immense as to endanger all life for miles around. Alas, even with enough flammable material to burn a small city, the fire lasted but minutes. The next day brought more of the same, with napalm added for good measure. More fires started and again failed to burn the cargo. Before the tragedy was done, many more millions of gallons of oil had coated Brittany, where the slick earned the epithet *la marée noire*.

Having failed to burn the oil, the British dumped several million gallons of detergents on it, both at sea and on beaches and cliffs; thousands of soldiers and volunteers went to work in a cleanup operation similar to Exxon's in Alaska. The French were opposed to the large-scale use of detergents, preferring to sink the oil instead. Scientists later discovered that the detergents, themselves quite toxic, did more harm than good to the environment; also, oil driven to the bottom by sinking agents smothered bottom-dwelling organisms. (Today's dispersants are less toxic, but they break up oil into finer particles in the water.

Thus, rather than ending the contamination, they make the oil more available to sea life. Scientists are trying to turn this to advantage with a developing class of genetically engineered microorganisms that can metabolize oil.) As *Oil in the Sea*, published by the National Academy of Sciences, aptly notes, "Many of the impacts observed were due largely to the awesome cleanup efforts used and not to the spilled oil." Although no trustworthy estimates exist of the amount of *Torrey Canyon* oil that was recovered in the cleanup effort, experts agree that it was paltry.

Other Spills

The *Torrey Canyon* story is unusually dramatic, but its outline is typical of spills and cleanups of that magnitude. In 1968, for example, the *General Colocotronis* spilled more than 2 million gallons of crude oil off Eleuthera, in the Bahamas. In 1969 an oil-well blowout dumped at least 1.3 million gallons into the waters near Santa Barbara, California, little of which was recovered. In 1970 the *Arrow* spilled 2.5 million gallons of oil into Chedabucto Bay, Nova Scotia, most of which luckily was swept out to sea. In 1976 the *Argo Merchant* disgorged onto the Nantucket shoals, off Massachusetts, about 7.5 million gallons, much of which stayed on the surface, turned into petroleum pancakes, and floated into the Atlantic. In 1978 the *Amoco Cadiz* lost 68 million gallons, contaminating 180 miles of Brittany, with much of the oil turning into a gooey, long-lasting, and toxic "mousse." In 1979 and 1980 the Ixtoc I well blowout in the Gulf of Mexico bled from 130 to 430 million gallons of oil over a nine-month period; optimistic estimates are that 10 percent was recovered. In June 1989, just a few months after the *Exxon Valdez* grounding, three large spills occurred within twelve hours: the *World Prodigy* leaked 420,000 gallons off Narragansett, Rhode Island; a barge in the Houston Ship Channel lost 250,000 gallons; and the *Presidente Rivera* spilled 800,000 gallons into the Delaware River. In 1990 the *America Trader* spilled 400,000 gallons near Huntington Beach, California.

In all these calamities only the cleanup of the *General Colocotronis* spill could be considered even a qualified success. After the *Colocotronis*, which was under charter to Humble Oil, a subsidiary of Standard Oil of New Jersey (now Exxon), ran aground, a dramatic lightering operation ("lightering" is transferring cargo to another vessel) retrieved nearly 3.5 million of 5.5 million gallons of oil in the ship's cargo, though the ship ultimately had to be scuttled. The best estimates are that "only" 14 to 20 percent of the *Colocotronis*'s oil spilled, polluting "only" a few miles of beach because most of the oil blew out to sea.

Even if one considers this a success story, human intervention had little to do with minimizing the damage. Luck, plainly, is our most effective guardian against shoreline contamination from major spills.

Technology Cannot Reduce Harm Caused by Spills

The random nature of oil tanker accidents, combined with financial constraints, makes it nearly impossible to ensure that sufficient containment equipment will be immediately available at the site of an oil spill. While contingency plans claim that barrier booms effectively impede the diffusion of oil, this technology is wholly ineffective in cases involving turbulent water. Major oil spills are usually accompanied by heavy storms and rough seas rather than the relatively calm waters anticipated by emergency-response planning scenarios. And skimming devices are mechanically unable to recover more than a small fraction of the discharged petroleum from the sea surface. . . .

The transport of oil by tankers is a tremendously complex technological and administrative undertaking, subject to occasional, inevitable failures.

When the next spill occurs, we will again be subjected to now-familiar industry claims: Such events are extraordinary, mitigation technologies are effective, impacts are transitory. We should insist on the truth.

Maurie J. Cohen, *The San Diego Union-Tribune*, January 20, 1993.

Were all these cases overloaded with conditions that hindered effective response? Perhaps they are stories of organizational and technological failure not because effective response to big spills is impossible but because conditions were simply too severe to permit any productive response: the seas were too high, the winds too violent, the catastrophe too sudden and remote. Such an argument raises the question of what would happen if conditions were more forgiving. In 1987 the Canadian Coast Guard, Environment Canada, and the Minerals Management Service of the U.S. Department of the Interior ran an experiment "to evaluate," in the words of two authors of a report on the project, "the containment and recovery capabilities of three state-of-the-art booms and skimmers."

The experiment, which cost nearly a million dollars, was run in the North Atlantic some twenty-five miles east of Newfoundland, where the researchers dumped about 20,000 gallons of oil. (They had a Canadian permit that required, among other things, westerly winds: the test was also scheduled for a season when no birds or whales would be in the area.) The plan was to contain and collect as much oil as possible. Three booms, one behind another, were to be strung around the stern of the spilling vessel. Then the skimmers would be put to work.

On the day of the experiment the sea had long swells, topped with two- to four-foot whitecaps, according to estimates (the instrument that would have measured them accurately failed), and the winds were at ten to twenty knots. By 6:45 A.M. the necessary vessels were in place, the helicopters (important for coordination) were ready to go, and the first line of boom was strung. By 9:00 all the oil had been released into the first line of boom. Between 9:00 and 10:00, when media representatives were allowed to watch, the experimenters tried to pull the second line of boom into place, but every attempt resulted in the boom's twisting in on itself. By 10:30 wind was pushing oil over the first boom, and oil was leaking under it as well. Although the frequently twisting second boom was a disappointment, the authors of the report claim that all three booms were able to contain the oil, at least temporarily.

A "Gigantic Flop"

The oil was then towed around in the last boom for about an hour, so that the experimenters could test their ability to corral oil while heading into wind (they fared poorly, to no one's surprise). Then the winds stiffened a bit, to perhaps twenty knots, one of the tow boats started going too fast, and the oil was lost. The experimenters managed to get the first boom back in place and deployed the skimmers. "The first skimmer . . . was deployed and no measurable recovery was observed," according to the report. Other problems developed. Of the three types of skimmers tested, two experienced mechanical problems with the support arms that suspended them from the boat, with the result that both were "frequently submerged so that oil and water were washed into the sump of the skimmer." One of these skimmers enjoyed an "overall rate of oil recovery [of] 60 gallons per minute with unknown amounts of the recovery resulting from frequent partial submergence." As the report indicates, albeit opaquely, the skimmers were probably more useful as buckets than as vacuum cleaners. A third skimmer operated admirably during the test, recovering almost eighty-five gallons of oil a minute, though for some reason it was used only a short while before being brought back aboard. The first skimmer, which earlier in the experiment had been a complete failure, was redeployed after the oil had been treated with a chemical that made it sticky, and this time the skimmer recovered about fifty gallons a minute. Finally rough seas and a dark sky brought the experiment to an end.

156

Evaluations of the Newfoundland experiment were mixed and sometimes conflicting. Though the authors of the report cited above don't give an overall recovery rate, they claim that "the containment and recovery effort was one of the most successful on record." They do not, however, define success. Edward Tennyson, of the Minerals Management Service, one of the report's authors, told me he estimated recovery at 15 to 20 percent. A month after the test an official Canadian Coast Guard estimate claimed that 33 to 40 percent of the oil had evaporated and that another 33 percent had been lost to sheens, the rainbow-colored film that petroleum products leave on water's surface. The Canadian Coast Guard also claimed that 25 percent of the oil had been recovered, a truly enormous proportion for an open-sea spill. But others in the Canadian Coast Guard, and staff members of Environment Canada, say quietly that the overall recovery rate was closer to 10 percent and consider the experiment a "gigantic flop." The literature on the experiment leads a reader to one unavoidable conclusion: even under reasonably favorable conditions, with state-of-the-art equipment, state-of-the-art chemicals, sufficient trained personnel, well-coordinated organizations, and a completely predictable time of spill, effective oil recovery is, by any reasonable definition, simply impossible. As an observer noted in Jeffrey Potter's 1973 book, *Disaster by Oil*, "It isn't that oil has a mind of its own. It's as mindless as those who spill it. The trouble is the stuff just won't cooperate.". . .

An Illusion of Control

We probably will not put an end to the enormous efforts that go into planning for oil spills, because too many political and organizational interests depend on perpetuating an illusion of control. Our dependence on oil grows unabated; conservation becomes a priority item on big political agendas only when oil production is threatened by instability or upheaval among the oil-producing nations. As oil prices rise—and they inevitably will—production will increase, more tankers will be built, and more tankers will make unintended deliveries to the sea. The least we can do is demand a forthright discussion of the risks of oil development, and the inevitable disasters we will be asked to absorb.

"It is imperative that the United States begin to take steps toward determining who should own the ocean."

Establishing Property Rights for the Oceans Is Necessary to Reduce Pollution

Kent Jeffreys

Kent Jeffreys is director of environmental studies for the Competitive Enterprise Institute, a Washington, D.C., think tank that works to develop private property approaches to environmental problems. In the following viewpoint, Jeffreys argues that all nations feel free to pollute the oceans because no one nation "owns" the rights to them. If property rights could be applied to the oceans, he maintains, the owners would have more concern about the quality of the water and would be able to seek damages from anyone who polluted it. This property rights approach would, Jeffreys believes, protect marine life and coastal areas.

As you read, consider the following questions:

1. Why do some forms of property suffer from overuse or abuse, in the author's opinion?
2. What three aspects of property rights does Jeffreys believe are essential to develop market interactions concerning the ocean?
3. Describe the Pride of Derby case, and explain why the author believes it is a good example of how property rights can help reduce pollution.

Excerpted from Kent Jeffreys, *Who Should Own the Ocean?* Washington, DC: Competitive Enterprise Institute, 1991. Reprinted with permission.

Roll on, thou deep and dark blue Ocean—roll!
Ten thousand fleets sweep over thee in vain;
Man marks the earth with ruin—his control
Stops with the shore.

When Lord Byron penned these words, it may have seemed incredible that Man would ever dominate the ocean. Today, however, Man has extended his impact, if not his control, to the most remote reaches of the ocean. Millions of people depend on the resources of the sea for survival, millions more respect its poetic beauty and intimidating vastness. While there is a universal desire to protect the ocean from such threats as pollution, overfishing, and habitat loss, there is confusion as to the proper approach to employ. Concerned individuals continue to debate the relative merits of various marine resource management systems.

The World's Marine Resources Must Be Managed

This viewpoint focuses on the living resources of the seas, although the principles discussed herein are generally applicable to other resource management questions (and examples are given to illuminate a point or possibility). The need for better management of the world's living marine resources has been explored and documented by numerous conferences, hearings, international symposia and the like. The most common prescriptions include international bans on fishing, limits on access to fishing areas and restrictions on equipment and fishing gear. While each of these proposals have distinct merits, they all revolve around the central issue that often remains unaddressed: *Who should own the ocean? . . .*

While the world's living marine resources are vast, they are not limitless. The estimated biomass of the world's oceans is approximately 100 billion tons. In comparison, the terrestrial portions of the globe (less than half the size of the oceans) maintain about ten times that amount. According to the United Nations Food and Agriculture Organization (FAO) the commercial harvest of ocean fisheries has risen from an estimated 19.8 million metric tons in 1950 to over 98 million tons today. An additional 24 million tons annually is taken by local fishermen. Proper management of each resource is important if people are to maximize the human and ecological benefits in a sustainable manner.

The Property Rights Concept

Territoriality is common in the animal kingdom, but property rights are a uniquely human characteristic. In essence, property rights comprise a spectrum of rules which govern human resource use. The literature on property rights has focused on two basic approaches to ownership: ownership in common and ownership by individuals. However, it is important to note that a single line cannot divide the various forms of property ownership into neat units. Although "ownership" implies complete control over a resource, that is not always the case.

For example, Francis T. Christy distinguishes "common property" by the nature of control over access rather than the identity of the owners and points out the fact that much of the "public" land in America is treated as private property through contractual arrangements with the governmental owner. S.V. Ciriancy-Wantrup and Richard C. Bishop distinguish "common property" and property held by "tenancy in common." As to the former, multiple owners will have equal rights to use the resource but this does not imply that each owner will hold an identical percentage interest in the resource. The authors also criticize the practice of equating an unowned resource (such as the high seas) with the "common property" concept.

More recently, Elinor Ostrom has examined the traditional methodology, which assumes that resource management must be entirely governmental or entirely private, and found that this does not correspond to real world situations. The author finds that permitting individuals to privately contract over resource use can lead to equitable and efficient arrangements utilizing an array of enforcement mechanisms. Ostrom concludes that "policies based on metaphors can be harmful."

Difficulties in Applying Property Rights to the Ocean

Although terrestrial treatment of property rights has dominated academic investigation, the principles of land-based tenure systems are generally applicable to marine situations. The difficulty arises from the physical and technological challenges confronting those attempting to extend property rights to the marine environment. Similar difficulties have resulted in the poor environmental quality of many river systems and airsheds.

The reason that some forms of property suffer from overuse or abuse is that control over access to the property resource is somehow prevented or rendered ineffective. In the ocean context, this has been the result of both political policy and the physical impracticality of enforcement of rules governing restricted access.

The original state of ownership of property, as well as its transferability, is determined by social institutions. These institutions, which include governmental institutions, determine whether ownership is shared in common or privately held by individuals. Most governmental activities in America, such as the police and judicial systems, are primarily concerned with property rights in some fashion, whether these rights are public or private in nature. Thus, defining and protecting property rights should be seen as the foundation of any societal effort to order economic activities.

Of course, perfect economic efficiency will not be found in any human endeavor, regardless of the property arrangements. The goal should be to select (or permit) the economic arrangements that most fully and efficiently provide for society's needs. In this regard current economic debate has shifted from a focus on guidance through government action toward a recognition of the efficacy of markets. Milton Friedman has said that "markets exist even in Albania." Nevertheless, crucial to their effectiveness is the type of governmental infrastructure within which markets are allowed to operate. In addition to a sound political infrastructure, efficient markets rely upon privately owned goods (property) that can be transferred to others through voluntary exchange.

Creating Legal Agreements

Three critical aspects of property rights must be present in order to enable them to facilitate efficient and equitable market interactions. These prerequisites are that the rights be clearly defined, defended against challengers, and transferable, in whole or in part, to others through voluntary exchange. The detailed terms of these transfers to others are the basis of contracts, legally enforceable agreements.

Although resources vary across space and time, human interactions have been remarkably consistent for centuries. Anthropologists have been able to document the attitudes and practices of coastal cultures around the globe. Interestingly, most have utilized a property rights approach to managing coastal resources. The property rights are not necessarily limited to an identified individual, but may be owned by kinship or tribal groups. Societal structures operate to identify the decision-maker for the particular resource in question. In this manner they have been able to deal with many of the same problems—albeit on a smaller scale—that face marine resource managers today. . . .

Adapting Property Rights to the Ocean

Although market terminology has become widely used in economic analyses, "markets" mean various things to various people. Many "market" solutions being proposed for environmental problems are not based on private ownership of any resource (e.g., a river) but are instead a shift in the treatment of the resource by its governmental "owner." If the preexisting conditions were sufficiently poor, even this can result in a significant improvement in resource management. True markets, however, do not exist without defensible private property rights.

Coastal regions, now often referred to as "coastal oceans," in contrast to the high seas, generally have been regarded as private property of one sort or another. Primarily, this has been the result of proximity to the claimant and the relatively easier task of enforcing the claim. Even out of sight of land, reefs and other identifiable features, such as upwellings of nutrient-rich water, have permanent locations, attracting numerous species of fish. These fishing spots are often treated as the private property of a single individual or select group. Even in the absence of governmental recognition of a property right, the privately held knowledge of an experienced fisherman can act to give exclusive control of the resource to an individual.

An Evolving Perception of the Ocean

While many societies historically implemented property rights regimes for coastal resources, through most of human history the open ocean was unowned, unexplored, and unimportant to most individuals. With the advent of ocean exploration and commerce, the legal treatment of the sea became an important issue for many nations. Today's international treatment of the oceans as a resource owned in common by all nations is a result of the five hundred year old struggle among international interests striving to control the ocean's resources. . . .

The justification for state control over marine resources can be based on two theories. First is the belief that government should own all things that have not been otherwise reduced to private possession, such as the oceans. However, as technology advances this justification will become less important, as the relative costs of private ownership are likely to decline substantially. The second justification is that government must play a role as trustee over marine resources for the benefit of all its citizens. Thus, it may be said that "the people" own the ocean, with the state as a managing trustee.

Thus, distribution of the resources to private individuals may become a *duty* of government where it can be shown that this would result in resource management superior to the existing arrangements.

It appears that for as long as mankind has taken food from the sea, property rights have been used to define and defend the resource. For example, in Denmark, farmers adjacent to the coastline have an ancient right to lay eeltraps. This right enables them to control access and secure rent. If property rights have been historically successful, then a property rights approach merits serious consideration as a solution to the problem of marine resource depletion. This is not to imply that there is no role for government. Government involvement may be necessary to enforce private contracts and property allocations, even when it played no significant role in their negotiation. . . .

Establishing Ownership of the Seas

One of the most important—and difficult—issues in marine resource management is that of pollution. The difficulty of persuading sovereign nations to restrict pollution which impacts a common fishery resource is readily apparent. Some commentators have argued that governmentally directed investments in pollution control can create sufficient benefits to satisfy the investing society even in the face of "free riders" who take advantage of the resulting improvements without contributing to the effort. Without careful coordination between nations—admittedly a difficult process—environmentally destructive behavior may be beneficial to uncooperative countries in the short term.

It can also be argued that the lack of strongly defined and defended property rights has permitted pollution of the coastal ocean regions. In actual practice, where water-based resources can be privately owned, private defenders of the resource can establish legal precedents to ward off future resource abuse. In theory, vital ecological habitat can be protected by the same legal mechanisms that enable shop and homeowners to prevent trespass or property damage.

The Pride of Derby

Consider water pollution in the context of a single river drainage basin. One of the most celebrated of such instances was the Pride of Derby case in England of 1951. The English Common Law had long permitted private legal actions against polluters. Cases against polluters were simply the logical extension of Common Law protection against trespassing and the creation of nuisances (which interfere with the "quiet enjoyment" of property ownership): "The Common Law entitles every riparian owner to have the water flowing past his land in its natural state of purity, and every fishery owner is entitled to the free movement of fish up and down a river from the sea to the source. Any denial of rights can be restrained by injunction and be the subject of a claim to damages."

Unfortunately, the costs of these civil legal actions were often prohibitive and nearly 100 years passed during which there were no cases taken to the British High Court to stop water pollution. Criminal statutes against water pollution had been passed by Parliament as early as 1876 but these required the local government authorities to prosecute the polluters. Since the local governments were, in fact, almost always the largest polluters (generally because they owned and operated ineffective sewage plants) there was more than a little reluctance to seek criminal sanctions.

The Anglers' Co-operative Association (a group of fishing club members), or A.C.A., was formed in 1948 and among its first acts was a request for an injunction against a water polluter under the Common Law. The resulting case included a damages award to the A.C.A. and began a trend toward private enforcement of the Common Law against polluters. The A.C.A. represented the Pride of Derby Angling Club and the Derby Angling Association against three major corporations that had been polluting the River Derwent and the River Trent. The suit was successful and the A.C.A. has continued to represent local member organizations in over 1500 cases. Today, most cases are settled out of court. The A.C.A. has noted that it was fighting pollution twenty years before the public and politicians became aware of the threat from water pollution. . . .

An Evolutionary Process

The oceans, along with the atmosphere, still present the most difficult (conceptually and physically) problems for a property rights based analysis. Clear and defensible private ownership has been either technologically impossible or prohibitively expensive. This impasse has led many observers to conclude that property rights approaches are inappropriate for global environmental issues—especially the so-called "pure" property rights approach of private, individual ownership of portions of any global resource.

No one expects universal private property rights to marine resources to be embraced overnight. But there are several avenues along the road to private ownership that hold promise for improving our treatment of marine fisheries. The example of . . . the Pride of Derby type of private protection mechanism points to the value of incorporating property rights approaches in our marine fisheries policies. . . .

The development of oceanic property rights must be an evolutionary process. There will not be an overnight shift to a new management regime. Nonetheless, an attempt should be made to improve the regulatory program through greater reliance upon individual decision-makers. A property rights approach can empower individuals to protect and utilize fishery resources simultaneously, and thereby allow sustainable resource utilization into the future. It is imperative that the United States begin to take steps toward determining who should own the ocean.

"The Coast Guard should be applauded for their efforts to carry out their missions with the resources they have."

Increased Funding for the Coast Guard Is Necessary

Frances Raskin

The U.S. Coast Guard is the government agency charged with protecting the nation's marine environment. In the following viewpoint, Frances Raskin supports the environmental work of the Coast Guard and proposes that the agency's funding be increased. The Coast Guard is an invaluable asset for cleaning up pollution such as that caused by the 1989 *Exxon Valdez* oil spill, the author contends. She states, however, that the agency's ability to respond to environmental crises has been harmed by lack of funding. Raskin concludes that increased support for the agency is needed to protect the oceans. Raskin is a writer for Friends of the Earth, an environmental organization based in Washington, D.C.

As you read, consider the following questions:

1. What lessons did the Coast Guard learn from the *Exxon Valdez* spill, according to the author?
2. What does VTS stand for, and why is it important, in Raskin's opinion?
3. Why are the Coast Guard's strike teams so valuable, in the author's opinion?

From Frances Raskin, "Can the Coast Guard Make Ends Meet?" *Friends of the Earth*, October 1990. Reprinted with permission.

While most of the nation cheered Congressional passage of the omnibus oil spill law, some environmentalists and U.S. Coast Guard officials began to worry. Can the agency handle increased oil spill response and prevention responsibilities without additional funding for equipment and personnel?

"The worst case is that we'll get the responsibility in the oil spill legislation, but Congress will give us no new money through the authorization and appropriations process," said Coast Guard Rear Adm. Joel Sipes, who heads the agency's Marine Environmental Protection program.

It's not a new predicament for the Guard, which is the lead agency charged with protecting the marine environment, but is also responsible for everything from fighting drug smugglers to responding to weekend sailors in distress.

"The Coast Guard should be applauded for their efforts to carry out their missions with the resources they have," said Clif Curtis, Director of Friends of the Earth's Oceanic Society Project. "Unfortunately, their responsibilities are constantly expanding. They are handed one mission on top of another but they haven't been given the money it takes to properly carry out these missions."

Weakened Programs

Coast Guard funding began to diminish early in the Reagan Administration, as the agency was engulfed in a wave of budget cuts. Among the budget victims were the Guard's "Vessel Traffic Services" (VTS)—meant to prevent ship collisions and groundings—which were cut or only partially completed. Money for research and development of oil spill cleanup methods and equipment became scarce. The Atlantic spill response "strike team" was eliminated, leaving only two teams—in Mobile, Alabama and north of San Francisco, California—to provide expert cleanup assistance.

Then, hard on the heels of the cutbacks, the *Exxon Valdez* gushed 11 million gallons of thick, black crude into the pristine waters of Prince William Sound, Alaska. Although the Coast Guard was praised for their efforts in salvaging and removing the oil from the wounded tanker, the March 24, 1989 spill brought to light the Coast Guard's many weakened programs. Post-accident reviews found some clear lessons to be learned from the Guard's role in the spill:

• To respond to spills quickly, the agency needs more strike teams.

• Experts said current cleanup and containment methods are effective only in good weather and calm waters.

• Surveys found that many ports lack systems to warn vessels of navigational hazards or possible collisions.

• Experience showed that the agency cannot adequately conduct all required vessel inspections.

The oil spill bill addresses some of these issues and "authorizes"—but cannot actually "appropriate"—additional funding to help the Guard carry out the reforms. But the Guard's Adm. Sipes is worried that the money may never materialize. He is not alone—environmentalists and lawmakers are also asking Congress to appropriate more funds. . . .

Coast Guard Blamed for *Valdez* Problems

The budget problem only adds to the Coast Guard's woes as they continue to struggle with the issues raised by the *Exxon Valdez* accident—which some officials say the agency may have been able to prevent. After a 16-month investigation, the National Transportation Safety Board said the Coast Guard's failure to adequately monitor the *Exxon Valdez* on its VTS when the ship left regular transport routes was partly to blame for the spill.

Marine Environmental Response

The Coast Guard is responsible for enforcing the Federal Water Pollution Control Act and various other laws relating to the protection of the marine environment. Program objectives are to ensure that public health and welfare and the environment are protected when spills occur. Under these laws, U.S. and foreign vessels are prohibited from using U.S. waters unless they have insurance or other guarantees that potential pollution liability for cleanup and damages will be met.

Other functions include providing a National Response Center to receive reports of oil and hazardous substance spills, investigating spills, initiating subsequent civil penalty actions when warranted, encouraging and monitoring responsible party cleanups, and when necessary, coordinating federally funded spill response operations. The program also provides a National Strike Force to assist Federal On-Scene Coordinators in responding to pollution incidents.

The United States Government Manual, 1991/1992.

Originally, the VTS in Prince William Sound was designed to monitor vessels until they reached the open sea. But lack of funding required the system to be scaled back, and at the time of the *Exxon Valdez* spill, the VTS covered approximately 25 percent of its intended range. Since the spill, the Coast Guard has expanded the VTS but officials admit they still don't have the money to complete the system.

Currently, only five ports have large-scale VTS systems—Prince William Sound, Puget Sound, San Francisco, Houston/Galveston, and Berwick Bay, LA. Most of the nation's busiest ports—including Los Angeles/Long Beach, Boston, Hampton Roads, VA, and New Orleans—do not have VTS systems. The VTS in New York Harbor—eliminated during a budget crunch in 1988—is being restored. And the Coast Guard is currently examining the need for traffic systems in another 23 ports.

"The sad thing is that for the price of cleaning up the *Exxon Valdez* accident ($2 billion), we could have put a VTS system in every major port in this country and still have $1 billion left over," said one shipping industry insider. But, analysts say, even improved VTS coverage will never entirely prevent accidents.

Improving Cleanup

Oil spill experts are now focusing on improving cleanup technology—no more than 10 to 15 percent of the oil in most major spills is recovered, according to Government Accounting Office estimates. However, funding for the Coast Guard's research and development program for cleanup technologies has dropped off in recent years—from $8.8 million in 1983 to barely more than $1 million in 1989.

"Cleanup must begin within hours of a spill," said Walter Parker, head of the state-appointed Alaska Oil Spill Commission in charge of investigating the *Exxon Valdez* cleanup. "The first 72 hours are critical. After that time, the oil starts washing up on the beaches—sometimes even sooner in narrow ship channels. The Coast Guard must have the capability to have their strike teams at the scene within that time frame, preferably within the first 24 hours."

To solve the problem of delayed response caused by long distances that often separate strike teams from spill sites, the new legislation calls for strike teams in each of the Coast Guard's ten districts. But agency officials say Congress must fund the new facilities and equipment, as well as approximately 600 additional personnel.

If the strike teams are not adequately funded, they say, the most likely source of manpower will be the vessel inspection program—already one of the Coast Guard's smallest and most overextended programs. In the last decade, inflation has outpaced funding for the Marine Safety Program, which includes commercial and recreational vessel inspection, as well as licensing and investigative activities. In fact, the program's budget for 1990—$143.8 million—was even smaller than it was in 1984.

With only 220 inspectors—who look for safety violations, faulty equipment, and structural failures such as poor welds and cracked hulls—the Coast Guard examines over 43,000 vessels annually. Most inspectors put in 70-hour work weeks. According to a Coast Guard survey, many inspectors admit that lack of manpower has resulted in "short-cutting . . . doing a barely adequate job on inspections instead of the more thorough job that was done in the past."

A Conflict of Interest

The shortage of qualified personnel has led the agency to pass on many of the inspections to "classification societies"—industry-supported organizations that set standards for ship design and construction. But allowing classification societies to conduct inspections may create a conflict of interest, critics say. Such inspectors are acting on behalf of both the owners and the government and may encounter pressure from owners to complete exams too quickly.

In 1987, the *Stuyvesant*—an oil tanker owned by Bay Tankers Co. of Englewood Cliffs, New Jersey—released 31,000 barrels of oil into the Gulf of Alaska in two spills. Both occurred as a result of cracks in the ship's hull. Although it is not certain the second structural failure would have been detected by inspectors, the vessel was allowed to sail without an extensive inspection after repairs were made to seal the crack that caused the first spill.

Many of the shortcomings in the Coast Guard's vessel inspection and spill response programs can be attributed to massive funding cuts that swept through the entire Marine Environmental Safety and Protection Division in the 1980s. Officials estimate they will need an additional $200 million to carry out the division's newly expanded responsibilities.

"More money needs to be available," said Rear Adm. Sipes. "We will continue to do the best we can to get the job done. But without more money, other programs will have to be cut or else we'll have to limit what we do."

"Fertilizers, pesticides, oils, solvents—all of it goes into the ocean."

Ending Ocean Dumping Is Necessary to Reduce Pollution

Jim Hogshire

Because the earth's oceans are so vast, many nations believe they can dump huge amounts of human waste, toxic chemicals, oil, garbage, and medical wastes into the oceans without causing environmental harm. In the following viewpoint, Jim Hogshire states that the oceans are not as resilient as many people believe. Ocean pollutants poison shellfish, ruin beaches, and destroy reefs, Hogshire maintains. Ocean dumping is a serious problem that must be addressed if the oceans are to remain healthy and pristine. Hogshire is a free-lance writer and contributor to the *Animal's Agenda*, a monthly publication dedicated to protecting the rights of animals.

As you read, consider the following questions:

1. Why does the author disagree with the official estimates of the amounts of sewage and waste dumped into U.S. rivers and coastal waters?
2. How does oil damage fish, according to Hogshire?
3. How are reefs harmed by ocean pollution, in the author's opinion?

From Jim Hogshire, "Sea of Troubles: Are We Deep-Sixing the Oceans?" *The Animals' Agenda*, June 1990. Reprinted with permission.

All garbage goes to the sea. Every bottle of drain opener, every toilet flush, every leaking drum of benzene. Landfills seep into rivers and industry sticks drainage pipes right into the water where everything from acid to zinc gets drawn away in a swirl of polluted brine. Smokestacks vomit tons of particulates into the atmosphere that end up in the ocean, either by rain or by first being strained through our bodies.

In 1989, more than 16 trillion gallons of sewage and industrial waste were dumped into rivers and coastal waters around the United States. The poisons have already forced the closing or restricting of 40 percent of U.S. shellfishing areas due to high levels of chemical or bacterial pollution. There is not a single major harbor, bay, or estuary in the continental U.S. that has not suffered damage or degradation.

Contaminated hospital waste, AIDS infected syringes, and raw human feces have washed up on public beaches, where disgusted bathers pick their way through all manner of trash, some of it brought ashore around the necks of strangled marine mammals.

Robert Sulnick, executive director of the American Oceans Campaign, which sponsors efforts to limit ocean damage, is dissatisfied with the figure of 16 trillion gallons of waste.

"That 16 trillion gallons is a conservative figure," he says. "The U.S. has no standards for measuring toxics, so we have no figures on the gallons or tonnage of toxics that go into the ocean on a daily basis. Each household dumps tons of pollutants down drains and gutters. Fertilizers, pesticides, oils, solvents—all of it goes into the ocean."

Toxic Trash

Sulnick says that, in addition, America dumped 94,000 curies of radioactive waste into the ocean between 1946 and 1970, including 89,472 drums which are still unaccounted for. The figure also doesn't take into account the floating trash that has recently been showing up in the gullets of dead marine mammals. He says oil platform blowouts, pipeline failures, and tanker spills spread additional millions of gallons of pollutants into the oceans. An oil spill might provide news stories for a matter of weeks, but it goes on damaging the ocean for decades, not only killing all the marine life in the immediate area, but also keeping new life out.

"Oil is a serious toxin," says Sulnick. "At .005 parts per billion—that's a concentration like five drops in a swimming pool—it begins to impair a fish's ability to hunt, and can kill fish eggs. That concentration kills plankton, which is the basis for the food chain and source of the ocean's oxygen."

Sulnick says oil spills sink, staying in the water column for a long time before getting sucked up into the wetlands and, ultimately, into our guts. "It's reached red line proportions," claims Sulnick. "It's like injecting poison into your bloodstream.". . .

The Coral Reefs

There may be no better example of the devastating impact human beings can have on the environment than the damage sustained by coral reefs. The one-two punch of greed and garbage simultaneously threatens the barrier reefs of the Caribbean, the Galapagos, Australia, Melanesia, the South China Sea, and the Bay of Bengal.

While ships—hugging the coastline to save fuel—smash into them, other people are busy detonating explosive charges on them. Any fish left alive are captured by tropical fish mongers who break off chunks of coral to get at their precious quarry. Still others merely break off pieces to hawk to tourists.

Ban Dumping

The deliberate dumping of garbage, sewage sludge and industrial waste into the sea was commonplace until public outrage forced 65 nations to adopt the London Dumping Convention in 1990. The agreement prohibits dumping of radioactive and toxic waste; participants have also agreed to stop all industrial dumping by 1995. Dumping of sewage sludge and dredged silt from ports and harbors (loaded with heavy metals) should also be prohibited. It can be done. New York City, which dumps 5.3 million tons a year of sewage sludge into the Atlantic, agreed to stop dumping in June 1992. Countries that have refused to ratify the London agreement should be pressured to do so urgently by signatory nations—using economic carrots or sticks as necessary.

The New Internationalist, August 1992.

To ensure the tourists have plenty of white sandy beaches to loll on, dredging machines rake fresh sand from the deeper water off the coast and deposit it on the land, breaking up the coral reefs that lie in between.

What's left of the reefs is at the mercy of various pollutants. Fertilizers run off from lush Miami lawns to feed algae colonies that steadily replace reefs. Silt builds up on the reefs, starving them of sunlight. Heavy metals from paints and industrial waste poison reefs and fish alike.

There has been a general decline in coral reef health over the last ten to 15 years," says Professor Peter Glynn of the

University of Miami, who heads a study of the environmental impact of humans on Florida reefs. "Generally I would say that coral reefs are under retreat in all the world's seas, just as the tropical rain forest is in retreat."

Glynn is not the first to compare the reefs with the rain forest: threats to the reefs are similar, as are their human-made causes. And the reefs are, as one scientist put it, "the habitat for the majority of the food chain out there." According to Canadian scientist David Suzuki, coral reefs occupy only one percent of the ocean yet support at least 25 percent of all marine fish species. . . .

[According to Glynn,] "The reefs are subject to more and more pollution. High levels of sediment and nutrients favor the growth of algae that outcompete corals and so, slowly the bottom areas are taken over by other organisms—algae and sponges."

Thus coral, which thrives in a low-nutrient environment to provide a home for an abundance of fish, is replaced by algae and sponges that depend on sewage and fertilizer runoff for their sustenance—and provide a home to nothing else. . . .

A Gigantic Dumpster

It has become tritely axiomatic that human beings use the ocean as a gigantic dumpster. How will we stop? When we're not pouring waste into it, we seem to be gutting it for any possible profit, as driftnets denude the seas of every fish, dolphins head for extinction in tuna nets, and bombs destroy coral reefs so a day's fish can be harvested.

Government representatives profess outrage at footage of chemical goo lapping up on pristine shores or of struggling dolphins and dead whales, yet the laws they pass are little more than grandstand plays to the folks at home and, ultimately, all laws are unenforceable on the open sea. . . .

Sulnick says one way to fight the trillion tons of garbage flowing into the sea is to stop dumping it at home. Anybody can write a letter to the editor, nobody has to buy tuna.

And all of us can speak out.

Periodical Bibliography

The following articles have been selected to supplement the diverse views presented in this chapter.

Sharon Begley — "One Deal That Was Too Good for Exxon," *Newsweek*, May 6, 1991.

Ken Brower — *Omni*, "Earth" section, three-part series on the state of the oceans, April, May, and June, 1989.

David J. Fishman — "Reef Madness," *Discover*, January 1991.

Forum for Applied Research and Public Policy — Entire section on oil spills, Winter 1991. Available from the Executive Sciences Institute, 1005 Mississippi Ave., Davenport, IA 52803.

Barry Hillenbrand — "Resilient Sea," *Time*, January 25, 1993.

Human Events — "Mother Nature's Slick Operation Against Oil Spills," February 16, 1991. Available from 422 First St. SE, Washington, DC 20003.

Justin Lancaster — "1991 Global Report: Ocean Pollution," *Buzzworm*, January/February 1991.

Lisa Y. Lefferts — "Too Many Risks in the Sea," *E Magazine*, January/February 1993.

Kailen Mooney — "Swim at Your Own Risk," *The Amicus Journal*, Fall 1992.

The New Internationalist — Entire section on saving the sea, August 1992. Available from PO Box 1143, Lewiston, NY 14092.

Katherine Parsons — "The Birds," *Garbage*, November/December 1991.

William A. Rutala and David J. Weber — "Infectious Waste-Mismatch Between Science and Policy," *The New England Journal of Medicine*, August 22, 1991.

Michael Satchell — The Rape of the Oceans," *U.S. News & World Report*, June 22, 1992.

Michael Specter — "The World's Oceans Are Sending an S.O.S.," *The New York Times*, May 3, 1992.

Kurt Stehling — "The Ocean's Greatest Gift," *The World & I*, April 1993.

Jeff Wheelwright — "Muzzling Science," *Newsweek*, April 22, 1991.

Denise Allen Zwicker — "Unseen but Essential: The Role of Offshore Pipelines," *The Lamp*, Winter 1991. Available from the Public Affairs Dept., Exxon Corporation, 225 E. John W. Carpenter Freeway, Irving, TX 75062-2298.

For Further Discussion

Chapter 1

1. Why do Terry L. Anderson and Donald R. Leal believe that free market incentives are the best way to allocate water? What problems does Helen Ingram see in free market incentives? Of the two viewpoints, which do you believe is the most persuasive? Why?

2. Most people would agree that conserving water is a good practice. Yet author David Lewis Feldman maintains that conservation will not help the United States manage its water supply. Do you agree with him? Why or why not?

3. Farmers are often criticized for wasting water. Yet many farmers argue that they are using the water to produce something of value, while city dwellers are using it to water their lawns. Do you think Marc Reisner's criticism of farmers is justified? How does where you live—in the city or in a rural area—affect your opinion?

Chapter 2

1. *ChemEcology* is published by an organization of chemical companies, while the Natural Resources Defense Council is an organization dedicated to preserving natural resources. How do you think these affiliations affect the viewpoints presented by these two groups?

2. Explain the differing attitudes concerning government involvement in the environment as expressed by Jonathan C. Kaledin and William F. Jasper. What are benefits and detriments of government involvement, in your opinion?

3. Chemicals are an integral part of modern life: They help run cars, clean clothes, and heal people. Yet they are also the cause of much pollution. What lifestyle changes, if any, would you be willing to make to reduce the amount of chemicals used by society? (For example, would you pay extra for organically grown fruit? Would you give up using a car?)

Chapter 3

1. On the surface, it would seem that the seriousness of acid rain would be easy to measure. Yet scientists disagree on this point. Whose argument—that of Cheryl Simon Silver or Dixy Lee Ray—do you find most compelling? Why?

2. J. Laurence Kulp was director of research for the National

Acid Precipitation Assessment Program (NAPAP) from 1985 to 1987. Knowing what you now know about NAPAP, do you agree with his belief that the government legislation to address acid rain is unnecessary? Why or why not? How do you think his former position affects his opinion?

3. Advocates of market incentives believe companies that pollute should have the right to buy and sell their pollution rights. In essence, companies would be given the right to pollute to a certain level. Those that pollute less than they are allowed could sell their extra pollution rights to companies who pollute more than they are allowed. Explain why Terry L. Anderson and Donald R. Leal support this idea, while Claude Engle and Hawley Truax oppose it.

Chapter 4

1. James E. Mielke states that while oil spills do at first kill birds, fish, and sea mammals, they cause no long-term harm to the oceans. Some might say that these animal deaths are similar to the thousands of animals killed on America's roads every year: While the animals' deaths are tragic, they have no long-term impact on the environment and should not force humans to alter their behavior. Do you agree with this analogy? Or, after reading Wesley Marx's view, do you believe humans should alter their behavior to prevent oil spills? Explain your reasoning.

2. In his viewpoint, Peter Nulty describes ways to prevent oil spills. His suggestions would seem logical to many people. Yet Lee Clarke argues that suggestions such as Nulty's are pointless. Why does Clarke believe this? Which author is the most persuasive and why?

Organizations to Contact

The editors have compiled the following list of organizations that are concerned with the issues debated in this book. All have publications or information available for interested readers. For best results, allow as much time as possible for the organizations to respond. The descriptions below are derived from materials provided by the organizations. This list was compiled upon the date of publication. Names, addresses, and phone numbers of organizations are subject to change.

The Acid Rain Foundation, Inc.
1410 Varsity Dr.
Raleigh, NC 27606
(919) 828-9443

The foundation was established to raise the level of public awareness about acid rain. It publishes the quarterly newsletter *Update* and the annual *Resource Directory.*

American Council on Science and Health (ACSH)
1995 Broadway, 16th Fl.
New York, NY 10023-5860
(212) 362-7044

ACSH is an association of scientists and doctors concerned with public health. It works to calm the fears of American citizens who believe their air, water, and food are contaminated. The council believes that existing regulatory controls protect the public from harm and that the environmental crisis is exaggerated. It publishes a series of pamphlets, including *Pesticides and Food Safety*, occasional special reports, and the monthly journal *ACSH News and Views.*

American Water Works Association (AWWA)
666 W. Quincy Ave.
Denver, CO 80235
(303) 794-7711

AWWA is an association of water utility managers, engineers, chemists, bacteriologists, and other individuals interested in public water supply and quality. It develops and supports research programs in waterworks design, construction, operation, and water quality control. The association publishes booklets, manuals, reference materials, the monthlies *AWWA Journal*, *Mainstream*, and *Washington Report*, and the bimonthly *Waterworld News.*

Chemical Manufacturers Association (CMA)
2501 M St. NW
Washington, DC 20037
(202) 887-1108

CMA sponsors research on water pollution and other areas crucial to chemical manufacturers. It promotes safety, education, and the belief that modern society needs chemicals. The organization believes that industrial chemical production can be environmentally responsible. It publishes *ChemEcology* and *CMA News* ten times a year and makes available various booklets promoting the safe use of chemicals.

Competitive Enterprise Institute (CEI)
233 Pennsylvania Ave. SE, Suite 200
Washington, DC 20003
(202) 547-1010

CEI encourages the use of economic incentives and private property rights as tools to protect the environment. It advocates making the private sector responsible for the environment. Its publications include the monthly newsletter *CEI Update* and numerous reprints and briefs.

Earth Island Institute
300 Broadway, Suite 28
San Francisco, CA 94133
(415) 788-3666

Earth Island Institute is a nonprofit organization that focuses on environmental issues and their relation to such concerns as human rights and economic development in the Third World. The institute's publications include its quarterly *Earth Island Journal*.

Environmental Defense Fund (EDF)
257 Park Ave. South
New York, NY 10010
(212) 505-2100

EDF is a nonprofit environmental education and advocacy organization. EDF's staff of attorneys, scientists, and economists seeks solutions to a broad range of environmental and public health problems. The fund publishes materials on acid rain, air quality, biotechnology, and other topics. *Biotechnology's Bitter Harvest, Developing Policies for Responding to Climatic Change,* and *Chlorofluorocarbon Policy* are a few of the fund's publications.

Foundation for Research on Economics and the Environment (FREE)
4900 25th Ave. NE, Suite 201
Seattle, WA 98105
(206) 548-1776

FREE is a research and educational foundation committed to building a society of free and responsible individuals. It promotes reliance on the free market as the way to coordinate social, economic, and environmental activities. Its publications include the quarterly newsletter *FREE Perspectives on Economics and the Environment.*

Friends of the Earth Foundation
218 D St. SE
Washington, DC 20003
(202) 544-2600

Friends of the Earth is dedicated to the preservation, restoration, and rational use of the earth's resources. Some of the specific issues it addresses include tropical rain forest destruction, global warming, and coastal and groundwater contamination. It publishes the quarterly periodical *Atmospheres* as well as research reports and bibliographies.

Greenpeace
1436 U St. NW
Washington, DC 20009
(202) 462-1177

Greenpeace opposes nuclear energy and the use of toxins and supports ocean and wildlife preservation. It uses controversial direct action techniques and strives for media coverage of its actions in an effort to educate the public. It publishes the bimonthly magazine *Greenpeace* and many books, including *Radiation and Health, Coastline,* and *The Greenpeace Book on Antarctica.*

National Agricultural Chemicals Association (NACA)
1155 15th St. NW, Suite 900
Washington, DC 20005
(202) 296-1585

NACA comprises firms that produce agricultural chemicals like herbicides, pesticides, defoliants, and soil disinfectants. It contains legislative and regulatory departments and maintains committees on environmental management, public health, and toxicology. The association promotes the use of chemicals in farming. It publishes the periodic *Bulletin* and the bimonthly *Actionews.*

National Environmental Development Association
1440 New York Ave. NW
Washington, DC 20005
(202) 638-1230

The association is a coalition of individuals from organized labor, agriculture, and industry. It promotes a balance between environmental protection and economic concerns in the development of America's resources. The association publishes the quarterly newsletter *Balance.*

National Wildlife Federation
1400 16th St. NW
Washington, DC 20036-2266
(202) 797-6800

With more than six million members, the federation is one of the largest environmental organizations in the country. It encourages the intelligent management of natural resources, awards fellowships for graduate studies in conservation, publishes classroom materials, and produces the daily radio show "Nature NewsBreak." The federation's publications include the monthlies *Ranger Rick, Your Big Backyard, The Leader*, and the annual *Environmental Quality Index.*

Natural Resources Defense Council (NRDC)
40 W. 20th St.
New York, NY 10011
(212) 727-2700

The NRDC is a nonprofit activist group of scientists, lawyers, and lay people working to promote environmentally safe energy sources and protection of the environment. It publishes the quarterly *Amicus Journal*, the newsletter *Newsline*, and a bibliography of books concerning air quality, water resources, and land preservation.

Sierra Club
530 Bush St.
San Francisco, CA 94108
(415) 981-8634

Since 1892, the Sierra Club has worked to protect and conserve the natural resources of the Sierra Nevada, the United States, and the world. It publishes the weekly *National News Report*, the bimonthly *Sierra*, and numerous books and newsletters.

U.S. Department of the Interior
Fish and Wildlife Service
Publications Unit
18th and C Streets NW, Room 130
Washington, DC 20240

This government agency is responsible for the nation's public lands and natural resources and for protecting fish and wildlife. It publishes numerous reports and articles on water management, water pollution, and acid rain.

Water Education Foundation
717 K St., Suite 517
Sacramento, CA 95814
(916) 444-6240

The foundation is a nonprofit organization that provides material on water-related issues—including quality control and conservation—to legislators, educators, and the general public. It sponsors seminars, supplies brochures, and promotes water-use education. The foundation publishes the Layperson Guides series and the bimonthly *Western Water*.

The Wilderness Society
900 17th St. NW
Washington, DC 20006-2596
(202) 833-2300

Founded in 1935, the Wilderness Society is a national nonprofit organization devoted to preserving America's forests, parks, rivers, deserts, and shorelands. It initiates citizen action, lobbies Congress, and sponsors coalitions among various environmental groups to help them work together to protect the nation's natural resources. The society provides technical assistance to land managers and lawmakers and works to educate the public about environmental issues. It publishes an annual report and sponsors televised nature programs.

World Resources Institute (WRI)
1709 New York Ave. NW
Washington, DC 20006
(202) 638-6300

WRI is a research and policy institute that aims to accurately inform the public about global resources and environmental conditions, to analyze emerging environmental issues, and to develop creative yet workable environmental policies. It publishes a wide array of materials, including its annual *World Resources* and numerous papers.

Worldwatch Institute
1776 Massachusetts Ave. NW
Washington, DC 20036
(202) 452-1999

The Worldwatch Institute is a nonprofit research organization created to analyze and focus public attention on global problems, including environmental concerns. Funded by private foundations and United Nations organizations, its mailing list includes the names of politicians, scholars, and the general public. It publishes the Worldwatch Paper series, featuring *Air Pollution, Acid Rain and the Future of Forests, Mining Urban Wastes: The Potential for Recycling,* and *Defusing the Toxics Threat: Controlling Pesticides and Industrial Waste.*

Bibliography of Books

Terry L. Anderson and Donald R. Leal — *Free Market Environmentalism.* Boulder, CO: Westview Press, 1991.

Roger G. Barry et al. — *Global Change.* Tucson: University of Arizona Press, 1991.

E. Calvin Beisner — *Prospects for Growth: A Biblical View of Population, Resources, and the Future.* Westchester, IL: Crossway Books, 1990.

Melvin A. Bernarde — *Our Precarious Habitat: Fifteen Years Later.* New York: John Wiley & Sons, 1989.

Thomas Berry — *The Dream of the Earth.* San Francisco: Sierra Club Books, 1988.

Janet Biehl — *Rethinking Eco-feminist Politics.* Boston: South End Press, 1991.

Peter Borelli, ed. — *Crossroads: Environmental Priorities for the Future.* Washington, DC: Island Press, 1988.

F.H. Bormann and Stephen R. Kellert, eds. — *Ecology, Economics, Ethics: The Broken Circle.* New Haven, CT: Yale University Press, 1992.

Daniel B. Botkin — *Discordant Harmonies: A New Ecology for the Twenty-First Century.* New York: Oxford University Press, 1990.

Peter Brackley, ed. — *World Guide to Environmental Issues and Organizations.* London: Longman, 1990.

Anna Bramwell — *Ecology in the Twentieth Century: A History.* New Haven, CT: Yale University Press, 1989.

Frances Cairncross — *Costing the Earth: The Challenge for Governments, the Opportunities for Business.* Boston: Harvard Business School Press, 1992.

Larry W. Canter and Robert C. Knox — *Ground Water Pollution Control.* Chelsea, MI: Lewis Publishers Inc., 1985.

Larry W. Canter, Robert C. Knox, and Deborah M. Fairchild — *Ground Water Quality Protection.* Chelsea, MI: Lewis Publishers Inc., 1987.

Steve Chase, ed. — *Defending the Earth: A Dialogue Between Murray Bookchin and Dave Foreman.* Concord, MA: Paul and Co., 1991.

Robin Clarke — *Water: The International Crisis.* London: Earthscan, 1991.

Harlan Cleveland — *The Global Commons: Policy for the Planet.* Lanham, MD: University Press of America, 1990.

Barry Commoner — *Making Peace with the Planet.* New York: Pantheon Books, 1990.

Arsen J. Darnay	*Statistical Record of the Environment.* Detroit: Gale Research Inc., 1991.
Andrew A. Dzurik	*Water Resources Planning.* Savage, MD: Rowman & Littlefield, 1990.
Paul R. Ehrlich and Anne H. Ehrlich	*Healing the Planet: Strategies for Resolving the Environmental Crisis.* Reading, MA: Addison-Wesley, 1991.
Mohamed T. El-Ashry and Diana C. Gibbons, eds.	*Water and Arid Lands of the Western United States.* New York: Cambridge University Press, 1988.
David Lewis Feldman	*Water Resources Management.* Baltimore: Johns Hopkins University Press, 1991.
John Firor	*The Changing Atmosphere: A Global Challenge.* New Haven, CT: Yale University Press, 1990.
The Global Tomorrow Coalition	*The Global Ecology Handbook: What You Can Do About the Environmental Crisis.* Boston: Beacon Press, 1990.
Edward Goldsmith, Peter Bunyard, Nicholas Hildyard, and Patrick McCully	*Imperiled Planet: Restoring Our Endangered Ecosystems.* Cambridge: Harvard University Press, 1992.
Al Gore	*Earth in the Balance: Ecology and the Human Spirit.* Boston: Houghton Mifflin, 1992.
Robert Gottleib and Margaret FitzSimmons	*Thirst for Growth: Water Agencies as Hidden Government in California.* Tucson: University of Arizona Press, 1991.
Andrew Goudie	*The Human Impact on the Natural Environment.* Oxford, England: Basil Blackwell, 1990.
Lindsey Grant	*Elephants in the Volkswagen: Facing the Tough Questions About Our Overcrowded Country.* New York: W.H. Freeman, 1992.
Barbara Graves, ed.	*Radon, Radium, and Other Radioactivity in Ground Water.* Chelsea, MI: Lewis Publishers and National Water Well Association, 1987.
Norris Hundley Jr.	*The Great Thirst: Californians and Water, 1770s-1980s.* Berkeley & Los Angeles: University of California Press, 1992.
Helen Ingram	*Water Politics: Continuity and Change.* Albuquerque: University of New Mexico Press, 1990.
Martin Jaffe and Frank DiNovo	*Local Groundwater Protection.* Washington, DC: American Planning Association, 1987.
Eric P. Jorgensen, ed.	*The Poisoned Well: New Strategies for Groundwater Protection.* Washington, DC: Island Press, 1989.
John Keeble	*Out of the Channel: The Exxon Valdez Oil Spill in Prince William Sound.* New York: HarperCollins, 1991.

Jay Lehr, ed.	*Rational Readings on Environmental Concerns.* New York: Van Nostrand Reinhold, 1992.
Martin W. Lewis	*Green Delusions.* Durham, NC: Duke University Press, 1992.
Ralph Lutts	*The Nature Fakers.* Golden, CO: Fulcrum Publishing, 1990.
Wesley Marx	*The Frail Ocean: A Blueprint for Change in the 1990s and Beyond.* Chester, CT: The Globe Pequot Press, 1991.
Donella H. Meadows, Dennis L. Meadows, and Jorgen Randers	*Beyond the Limits: Confronting Global Collapse, Envisioning a Sustainable Future.* Chelsea, VT: Chelsea Green, 1992.
E.G. Nisbet	*Leaving Eden: To Protect and Manage the Earth.* New York: Cambridge University Press, 1991.
G. William Page, ed.	*Planning for Groundwater Protection.* San Diego: Academic Press, 1987.
Bruce Piasecki and Peter Asmus	*In Search of Environmental Excellence: Moving Beyond Blame.* New York: Simon & Schuster, 1990.
Gerard Piel	*Only One World: Our Own to Make and to Keep.* New York: W.H. Freeman, 1992.
Christopher Plant and Judith Plant, eds.	*Green Business: Hope or Hoax?* Philadelphia: New Society Publishers, 1991.
Giulio Pontecorvo	*The New Order of the Oceans.* New York: Columbia University Press, 1986.
Clive Ponting	*A Green History of the World: The Environment and the Collapse of Great Civilizations.* New York: St. Martin's Press, 1992.
Paul R. Portney, ed.	*Public Policies for Environmental Protection.* Washington, DC: Resources for the Future, 1990.
Sandra Postel	*Last Oasis: Facing Water Scarcity.* New York: Norton, 1992.
Dixy Lee Ray and Lou Guzzo	*Trashing the Planet.* Washington, DC: Regnery Gateway, 1990.
Walter V.C. Reid and Mark C. Trexler	*Drowning the National Heritage: Climate Change and Coastal Biodiversity in the United States.* Washington, DC: World Resources Institute, 1991.
Jeremy Rifkin	*Biosphere Politics: A New Consciousness for a New Century.* New York: Crown, 1991.
Annabel Rodda	*Women and the Environment.* London: Zed Books, 1991.

Theodore Roszak   *The Voice of the Earth*. New York: Simon & Schuster, 1992.

Dorion Sagan   *Biospheres: Metamorphosis of Planet Earth*. New York: McGraw-Hill, 1989.

Stephan Schmidheiny   *Changing Course: A Global Business Perspective on Development and the Environment*. Cambridge, MA: MIT Press, 1992.

Cheryl Simon Silver with Ruth S. DeFries   *One Earth, One Future: Our Changing Global Environment*. Washington, DC: National Academy Press, 1990.

S. Fred Singer, ed.   *Global Climate Change: Human and Natural Influences*. New York: Paragon House, 1990.

S. Fred Singer, ed.   *The Ocean in Human Affairs*. New York: Paragon House, 1990.

W. Edward Stead and Jean Garner Stead   *Management for a Small Planet*. Newbury Park, CA: Sage Publications, 1992.

Payson R. Stevens and Kevin W. Kelley   *Embracing Earth*. San Francisco: Chronicle Books, 1992.

Curtis C. Travis and Elizabeth L. Etnier, eds.   *Groundwater Pollution: Environmental and Legal Problems*. Boulder, CO: Westview Press, 1984.

E.O. Wilson, ed.   *Biodiversity*. Washington, DC: National Academy Press, 1989.

Oran R. Young   *International Cooperation: Building Regimes for Natural Resources and the Environment*. Ithaca, NY: Cornell University Press, 1989.

Index